Camels in Development

CAMELS IN DEVELOPMENT

Sustainable Production in African Drylands

Edited by

Anders Hjort af Ornäs

Scandinavian Institute of African Studies, 1988

Cover drawing: Camel cart from Jaipur, India

ISBN 91-7106-281-5

Printed in Sweden by
Motala Grafiska, Motala1988

Contents

Preface

The seminar "The case of African drylands and balanced camel production" was arranged by the Scandinavian Institute of African Studies (SIAS) as one activity within the research programme *Human Life in Arid Lands*. This research programme is financed by SAREC, the Swedish Agency for Research Cooperation with Developing Countries. It represents an effort by SIAS to concentrate attention on some of the major issues for Africa today.

This meeting was financed by NORAD or, rather, the Royal Norwegian Ministry for Development Cooperation, (Departementet for Utviklingshjelp). We acknowledge this support with gratitude along with a SAREC contribution that made it possible for a Latin American participant to attend.

One ambition from the SIAS side was to ensure that the meeting was dominated by Third World scholars. As the list of participants indicates, this was achieved. I would like to extend our gratitude to the participants. Thanks to their personal interest in camel rearing, we not only had interesting discussions during those three days, October 20-22 1987, but also ideas and suggestions to take back home. The meeting also initiated many contacts. One major achievement will most likely be a strengthened South-to-South cooperation around the seminar's theme.

The meeting took place at Furudal, near Rättvik in Sweden. The participants want to express their thanks to Lennart Öhnell for the extremely good organization and the friendly environment. Professor I. Eldisougi Mustafa expressed our gratitude by writing a poem in Arabic and providing a free translation into English, which follows the Arabic:

The O'Re forests, the so many mountains
and the gushing flushing water;
like thunder:
They all storm the happy heart of mine
with uncountable verses of thanks.
I am thus highly indebted
to the extent of being a prisoner.
The response to the she- and he-camels
was all around from all colleagues.

Welcome to colleagues from abroad
who laid aside the time when gushing armies
devastated the unarmed people.
At present, they raise, high up,
the flag of knowledge and science:
How will it then trigger the spirit for all of us.
Look at him, the one whose soul was taken
by the she-camel and its calf.
Look at him building an edifice of knowledge
for us and nomads in the desert.
Lennart has well taken all with pleasure as guests.
We will then forget any thoughts of wars.

Two more names have to be added to the list of acknowledgements: Susanne Linderos and Anne-Marie Vintersved, who acted as organizers and secretaries during the conference. They were the only women in the meeting, a fact which more reflects the male-dominated sphere of camel rearing than a chauvinistic Nordic attitude. Together with representatives of the Nordic aid organizations, I believe they became gradually fascinated by the potential of camel rearing, thanks to the enthusiastic participants. Anne-Marie Vintersved also typed the manuscripts for the present volume.

Uppsala, March 1988
Anders Hjort af Ornäs

Introduction

Anders Hjort af Ornäs

The Scandinavian Institute of African Studies (SIAS) arranged a seminar on October 20-22 1987 with the title "The case of African drylands and balanced camel production". The purpose was primarily to bring together a group of scholars from the Third World in order to exchange information about how the dromedary could play a role in sustainable food production in the arid tracts of Africa. In spite of this geographical focus, we sought to widen the scope by inviting scholars also from Asia and Latin America. The ambition was to turn the meeting more into concern of the South than the North.

The background to the problem formulation is of course the drought disasters, and the search for an improved food production in the form of milk and meat from arid and semi-arid lands. The seminar was intended to bring one asset, the dromedary or one-humped camel, into the picture. While doing so, we do not wish to suggest camel rearing as a universal remedy. But for limited parts of Africa the animal holds a promise for reliable food production, either through improving existing systems or within the framework of more intensive production systems.

This seminar is one in a range of activities at SIAS to look into the potential of the dromedary, mostly in cooperation with researchers from developing countries. Other efforts are a series of workshops held in camel rearing areas between herdsmen and national scholars. Also, some more specific research projects are undertaken in partnership with researchers from camel-rearing countries.

This volume reports on the above-mentioned seminar. Contributors are primarily from African countries, but a few other participants were invited in order to widen the range of experience. Thus all the members of the Camelidae family were discussed, at least for comparative purposes. (Since the seminar concerned Africa we assume in the text that follows that the term "camel" stands for dromedary unless stated otherwise.) The recommendations from the seminar emphasize the need for urgent attention to what many feel is a forgotten asset in arid and semi-arid lands. The emphasis on research work stems from a need for basic knowledge before actual development projects are implemented.

From an ecological perspective the camel is an extremely interesting domestic animal. It can endure hot climate and go longer without water than other species. It has big soft feet, so that the vegetation cover is not trampled. It browses in bush rather than grazes on a sparse grass cover. Its selective browsing behaviour means an even environmental "wear and tear", thus minimizing the danger of desertification. It is resistant to disease and gives great volumes of milk in comparison with all other domestic species in similar environments. The nutritional value of camel milk is high throughout the year, also during dry seasons. The milk is rich in Vitamin C, a fact that is unique and particularly welcome in arid areas, which are frequently struck by drought periods.

The seminar looked among other things at long-term possibilities for increased production of milk and meat in today's changing world. Special attention was given to the situation of the economically most vulnerable groups of people. The discussions took into account traditional rights to pasture and water, and how new techniques (land management, feeding, upgrading and disease control) influence production and man's capacity to maintain or obtain sustainable production.

The fact that living conditions need to be changed drastically for vulnerable persons leads to the question: how to find appropriate means to do so. Vulnerability is not a situation that the victims have created themselves; it should rather be seen as a general consequence of political and social circumstances. This is of course true also in situations where ecological imbalance is part of the picture.

Development projects with an environmental dimension touch the very foundation of man's existence: land, water, vegetation, livestock, labour. This means that such decisive issues as inequality between regions or individuals, ownership rights or the degree of sustainable subsistence are always present. The question of how to obtain ecologically-balanced living conditions has a social and a political dimension that can never be totally excluded from the picture. We are concerned with justice, participation and security both for individuals and nations.

Issues of political control and cultural variation, for example, need to be added to conventional thinking about man's ways of relating to the environment. We then have to make observations of both a specific and a general character.

An example of the former would be cultural variations in conceptions of "ownership" of land, livestock or products, or how food is distributed in a community. The change towards concentration of livestock ownership from pastoralists to townsmen illustrates the general trend to profound change in local communities. An economic and social stratification creates a potential for growth but it also adds increased vulnerability to the local community.

In the specific case, two groups may cooperate or compete over the exploitation of a tract of land. One illustration is the culturally institutionalized cooperation between Samburu and Rendille in Kenya. Members of one of these ethnic groups subsist from raising cattle that use mainly grassland for pasture. Members of the other group keep camels, which prefer bush. The cooperation evolves around use of pasture land within a mutual territory in a way that compensates for differences between cattle and camel herd growth through intermarriage, and around a need for redistribution of labour.

In many cases, however, groups compete rather than cooperate. Discussions then about human adaptation to ecosystems and optimum resource utilization become somewhat academic.

Much has been said over the last years about tree plantation and various forms of farming in those parts of the world where water is a scarce resource. But in certain regions there is a viable alternative for improved subsistence through livestock rearing. Camel herding under existing circumstances or in some sort of modified ranching system is receiving more and more attention.

The work during the seminar was structured into themes. The first session had the general heading *Camel management in Africa*. The discussion following the presentation of papers centred around the notion of sustainable food production and the quest for balanced production systems. Papers presented were both very general and specific (with reference to the Sudanese situation). There is an obvious conflict between the need to increase export of camels and the need for increased food production for local consumption. In Sudan a decisive issue is to secure meat and milk deliveries for increasing urban markets. A flowering network of middlemen create a problem for reliable deliveries, and this becomes a political question.

Another political issue is the complex task of achieving a balance between traditional systems and new ones. Existing production systems which provide food and supply local markets need to be improved. At the same time new systems for major urban and international markets seem to be needed. One of the key issues is how land is actually controlled.

Papers presented in this session were by Anders Hjort af Ornäs, I. Eldisougi Mustafa and Mohamed M.A. Salih. The discussant, Moses Awogbade, emphasized particularly the need to observe the inherent conflict between a national and a local perspective.

The second session concentrated on *The East African scene*, building on the Sudanese contributions in Session 1. The contributions from Djibouti and Ethiopia both dealt with the importance of land, and how one must distinguish between different kinds of arid environments. They also emphasized the significance of the camel in exchange relations and the importance of avoiding to consider camel herding in isolation from other activities.

The way that political circumstances affect camel management and environmental issues was noted on several occasions. However, we did not move into trying to formulate political answers to current problems; this was felt to lie outside the scope of the seminar.

Papers presented were by Mohamed A. Rirash and Ayele G. Mariam. The discussant, Frode Storås, emphasized the important role that the camel plays in many cultural traditions in the region. Along with the socio-cultural role comes the intricate adaptation to the harsh environment around the Horn of Africa. His views are included in the discussant's comments to Section 2.

The third section, *Camelidae management in Latin America and Asia*, added an interesting comparative dimension. The llama and alpaca of Latin America were presented by Julio Sumar, the Indian situation by N. D. Khanna and that in Abu Dhabi by Saeed S. A. Athera. The veterinarians found rather obvious fields for comparative work, especially on the methodological side such as breeds classification and mapping of ecosystems. In the discussion we also entered man's relations both to the domestic herds and more generally to the habitat. Thus we were brought back to the earlier issue of sustainable food production. N. Shanmugaratnam, the discussant for this Session, raised a number of points, emphasizing the role that social science has to play to remedy the under-researched field of camel pastoralism. The other important conclusion from this session was the potential for South/South cooperation; inputs from both Peru and India into research work in Africa seems highly promising. This becomes even more needed in the current situation, as the International Livestock Centre for Africa, ILCA, does not give priority to camel research.

Session number 4 focussed on *The Somali experience and its implications*. However, the session was introduced by a presentation of the Intergovernmental Authority on Drought and Development, IGADD, by its research director, Ahmed El-Houri. This organization was set up in January 1986 by the Foreign Ministers of Djibouti, Ethiopia, Kenya, Somalia, Sudan and Uganda.The organization hosts both regional and national projects.

The remainder of the session was dedicated to research in Somalia. Set Bornstein presented an overview of the role the camel plays as a domestic animal.The discussion posed the question about land utilization: Does intensified camel herding allow new and under-utilized tracts of land to become available? To what extent is overgrazing "man-made", i.e. caused by improper management of livestock? What is the capacity of feed lots for camels?

The paper by Mohamed A. Hussein and A. Hjort af Ornäs brought back the issue of the potential food production from extensively managed herds in the area; by analyzing age and sex structures of domestic herds one can foresee possible milk output, and also herd developments for the future. The discussant, I. Eldisougi Mustafa, also emphasized food production capacities of camel family herds. In his view the camel meat production for urban markets is one of the more significant contributions that can be made in the future. Much interest was attached to the Somali Camel Research Project, led by Mohamed A. Hussein and A. Hjort af Ornäs. Therefore this project is presented as an Annex to the present volume.

Session 5, on *The camel and development*, took us back to the overall theme of the seminar. The land issue again was brought to the fore by Moses Awogbade, who took up a number of relevant issues in connection with settlement schemes in Nigeria. Extensive herding practices are threatened by other land use systems. Dry season pastures are turned into farm land, utilized by "strangers" on settlement schemes; reserve pastures become game parks etc. The discussion returned to the potential of camel rearing as a worthwhile food production system, if properly managed. We then noted a range of quite practical conclusions whose essence is captured in the set of recommendations at the end. They concern the need for maintaining a contact network for the dissemination of both information and research cooperation. The group noted the special importance attached to the socio-economic side of keeping camels. Cooperation across national boundaries seems essential, and the newly established IGADD was welcomed as one possible body to achieve such a goal.

An Appeal for a Modified Camel Productivity

I. Eldisougi Mustafa

INTRODUCTION

The Arabic language is extremely rich in terms describing the camel. This
is clearly seen in the early Arabic poetry and the "Seven Odes" in particular. Why not? It is the animal that has continuously served as a mount and
a beast of burden in addition to providing bedouins and nomads with
food, clothing, shelter and ritual sacrifices. The flesh tastes somewhat like
beef (that of young camels is unrivalled) while the camel liver is considered a delicacy. The milk is nutritious, its high salt and vitamin C content
is badly needed for those whose travel in the desert exposes them to diseases and causes continuous sweating and loss of salt. The camel is as well
unrivalled in its productivity and ability to withstand thirst and survive on
the thorns of desert shrubs. Deep in the desert, where wood and kerosene
are never thought of, the dried pellets of camel manure are the only source
of fire.

It is thus relevant to give some examples of the names in Arabic. The
word "Ibil" is used as a collective Arabic noun indicating the dromedary
and the bactrian camel with two humps. "Djamal" is sometimes used
equally with "ibil" for the two species but it is mostly used for the male,
while the female is given the name "Naka". When the dromedary is five
years old it is called "ba'ir", a term mostly used for the male. "Ho'war" is
the name given to a sucking young camel and once weaned it is called
"Faseel". "Bakr" and "Bakra" are used respectively for the males and females of not less than two years of age; the male ready for mount at this
age is also called "Ga'oud".

THE CAMEL IN HOLY BOOKS

The reference to camels in the Old Testament is a clear indication of the
normal presence of domesticated camels in the Arabian peninsula before
the time of the prophet Abraham, i.e. approximately 1800 B.C. Genesis
12(16) reads: "He (the Pharaoh) treated Abram well because of her (Sarai),
and Abram came to possess sheep and cattle and asses, male and female

slaves, she-asses and camels". Genesis 24(10) reads: "The servant took ten camels from his master's herd", a clear reference to the dowry in camels paid by the prophet Abraham for the marriage of his son Isaac to Rebecca.

The camel in The Holy Kur'an is referred to in a number of verses. In Sura VI, the Arabic word "An'am" is used for the cud-chewing animals and as such further details are given in verses 143 and 144 where "ibil" (i.e. camels) are mentioned along with sheep, goats and cattle.

Sura VII (Al-A'raf) verse 73 refers to a wonderful she-camel belonging to Saleh (or rather Shelah), the son of Arphaxad the son of Sam (or rather Shem), son of Noah. The verse reads: "To the Thamud people we sent Saleh, one of their own brethren. He said: O, my people! Worship God; Ye have no other God but him. Now has come unto you a clear sign from your Lord. This she-camel of God is a sign unto you: so leave it to graze on God's earth and let it come to no harm". The Thamud people lived in Arabia Petraea and were succeeded later on by Nabataeans. They were mentioned in an inscription of the Assyrian king Sargon, dated 715 B.C. as the people of eastern and central Arabia. They became godless and arrogant and were destroyed by an earthquake and a hurricane. According to the same Sura VII (verse 77), they ham-strung the she-camel and insolently defied the Order of their Lord, saying "O, Saleh! bring about thy threats if thou art An Apostle of God. So the blasting wind took them unaware and in the morning they lay prostrate in their homes".

The she-camel was a symbol used by the prophet Saleh for warning the oppressors of the poor and the arrogant privileged classes who monopolized the springs and pastures. A special name for the sacrificial camels, "Boud'n", is found in verse 36 of Sura XXII (Al-Hajj i.e. Pilgrimage). It reads: "The sacrificial camels, We have made for you as among the symbols from God: In them is (much) Good for you: Then pronounce the name of God over them as they line up for sacrifice: When they are down on their sides (after slaughter), Eat ye thereof, and feed those who (beg not but) live in contentment and those badly in need due to hunger: Thus have We made animals subject to you that Ye may be grateful. It is not their meat nor their blood, that reaches God: It is your piety that reaches him".

Verse 17 of Sura LXXXVIII (Al-Gashiya or the Overwhelming Event) reads: "Do not they look at the camels "Ibil", How they are created? And at the Sky, How it is raised?" In this and the following three verses, human beings are asked to contemplate the creation of camels, the sky, mountains and the earth which they see in their everyday life. These are of high design and full of meaning. The animal mentioned is still the ship of the desert and the object of research in vogue in the twentieth century.

CAMEL LOCALITIES IN THE SUDAN

Sudan is a vast country where camel nomadism is widely practised. Approximately three million camels are grazing in a systematic migratory movement in search of pasture and water. They thrive mostly in the northwestern and northeastern parts of the Sudan. In the former part, the rainfall is very scanty and the land is a dry type of a steppe with sand dunes, patches of hills and stony outcrops. The tribes involved are mainly Kababbish, Zaggewa, Hawa'weer and Kawahla. The area is characterized by scattered acacia trees and scanty shrubs that provide possible grazing for camels. With the start of the early rains in the south, the camel caravans begin their southward movement in parallel lines to graze the new grass. When winter begins, the direction of the movement is reversed.

In the north-eastern part, there is no nomadic camel movement. Camels are found in the Red Sea hills and coastal plains and in the North-eastern desert stretching down to the Nile; also in the Butana clay plains. The tribes involved are the Beja, Bisharia and Rashaida. The latter raise a heavy type of camel, while the Amarar and Bisharia have an excellent light type of riding camel.

The gently rolling plains of Butana are inhabited by nomadic and semi-nomadic camel owners of the Shukriya tribe. Though mostly covered by a clay soil, this area also has sand and rocks. Further south, where more rain falls (300-500 mm), and the pasture is dominated by grass, acacia and a bigger variety of other trees. Here, cattle are also raised.

A MODIFIED CAMEL PRODUCTIVITY

Without infringing too much upon the social life of nomads, what are the possibilities of increasing camel productivity in an attempt to raise the standard of living? It is a formidable task, but not impossible. Such a big sector of the population cannot be ignored in the development plans of the country. At the same time, there is a false notion that nomadism as a way of life is detrimental to the economy and that the nomads have to be settled. Many who recently lost animals due to the drought and came to the cities and towns for work left again with the start of the rains last year. The nomads enjoy their way of life and will not give it up unless compelled to do so, although it means constantly adapting themselves to nature and to the seasons of the year.

With the increasing demand for meat and milk, it is necessary to re-assess camel productivity. Full use should be made of the animal's ability to thrive in arid areas and live on thorns and the rough coarse shrubs of the desert. The flavour and juiciness of camel meat are not only enjoyed by nomads and camel owners; for those of us who relish "Sheesh Kabab" or "Kofta", camel meat brings a special flavour.

CONCLUSION

Livestock in Sudan supplies most of domestic demand for animal products and allows a surplus to be exported as well, e.g. to Egypt, Libya and Saudi Arabia, although, some parts of the Sudan are still deficient in processed animal products.

With the introduction of modern technology, a lot could gradually be done, as follows:

1. Provision of wells at certain spots along the camel routes that use solar energy to pump the water.
2. The use of camels for ploughing and cultivation.
3. Creation of markets around the well where camels are traded for other goods.
4. Establishment around certain wells of slaughterhouses and factories to process camel meat and milk products along with hides, wool and poultry feed. Mobile veterinary and medical services could also be based at these oases.
5. Export of camels on the hoof should be stopped except for those light types used for racing.

The intention of these proposed measures is not a complete settlement of camel nomads. Education can be adapted to the nomadic way of life - as it was in the past, during the early propagation of Islam in north and central Africa. Teachers of religion Arabic lived then with the nomads and moved around with them.

REFERENCES

Al Mu'allakat Al Sab'aa (The Seven Odes)
M. Abdalla Al Sa'nia 1983: *Arabian Ibil*. Kuwait.
Gauthier-Pilters, H. and Dagg, A.I. 1981: *The Camel. Its Evolution, Ecology, Behaviour and Relationship to Man*. Chicago: Chicago University Press.
Knoess K.H. 1977: "The camel as a meat and a milk animal". *World animal Review*, 22.
Proceedings of the 10th Annual Conference of the Philosophical society of the Sudan, 11-12 January 1962, Khartoum.
The Glorious Kor'an, translation and commentary by Abdullah Yousif Ali, May, 1973.
The New English Bible with the Apocrypha. Oxford and Cambridge University Presses 1970.
Trimingham, J.S. 1959: *Islam in West Africa*. Oxford University Press.

Camel Production in the Arid Lands of the Sudan: National and Local Perceptions of the Potential

M.A. Mohamed Salih

The neglect of camel pastoralism in the Sudan is outrageous considering the potential of the arid lands and the recurrence of drought and famine. Furthermore, it is appalling that the question of what to do with those who depend on camels for food has been ignored by national planners.

Sudan is one of the leading African countries in keeping detailed records of the camel trade in the Livestock and Meat marketing Corporation and the Ministry of Commerce, where an official register of camel exports is found. There are also fine research results which have been compiled by the Camel Research Unit under the guidance of the National Council of Agricultural Research. This wealth of information and research findings lies dormant. Planners and administrators have so far failed to see the relevance of camel pastoralism to the traditional food system.

The present plans for socio-economic development in the Sudan do not hold any promise for balanced livestock or camel production. Sudanese planners have so far centred their efforts around agricultural expansion without any clear policy as regards livestock. Since the arid lands are characterized by ecological unpredictability, the common view is that the present form of pastoral life is well suited to the ecological conditions of camel pastoralism. This view is encouraged by international financing institutions, which consider cost recovery almost inconceivable in the harsh conditions of the arid lands. Here one can see that camel production is caught between two irreconcilable perceptions: the social needs of the population and the national planning demand for projects with high potential cost recovery, in the crudest economic sense.

The inventory of failure of pastoral development projects has much to do with the perceptions held by technicians and planners, who have made the pastoralists victims of technical experiments and unsuccessful settlement schemes.

The gap between national and local perceptions can be bridged if contact points are developed and development-considered from the point of view of those who are in need and most vulnerable to natural calamities. This is particularly important in the case of camel pastoralists, whose system of production is very susceptible to ecological catastrophes. The previous drought had shown that unchecked pastoral production can lead to overstocking and overgrazing, usually aggravated by ecological degradation. There is no evidence that herders with large herds were better off in confronting the drought than those who have what is considered a herd of optimum size, taking into account household composition and labour for herd management. Relief agencies report herd losses to be proportional to herd size. The death of millions of animals and the impoverishment of hundreds of thousands of households highlights the urgent need for a balanced system of production to shield pastoralists from mass starvation and death. This can be achieved either if food is locally produced when climatic conditions allow or with favourable conversion rates. This implies that the pastoral system should shift from herd accumulation to conversion. Nevertheless, this cannot be achieved without a positive governmental intervention where new policies are adopted and present constraints on pastoral production eliminated.

The search for a viable food system for the arid lands cannot be limited to camel pastoralism, since pastoralists are in most cases dependent on grain imports, especially during droughts. The difficulty in obtaining grain has recently been intensified by the pastoralists, incorporation into the market economy. Their dependence on grain and manufactured imports is aggravated by the limited demand for their exports on the international market and unfavourable terms of trade.

Unlike cattle herders, who roam wetter zones, camel pastoralists occupy the most marginal drylands in which grain cultivation (outside the oases) is impossible. They can easily become destitute in the event of prolonged drought.

Designing a balanced food system for camel pastoralists cannot depend only on the camel. It must take account of demographic factors and the socio-economic and political context. And it will be affected by the exchange value of camel products into cash or grain and other forms of goods and services. In the Sudan camel pastoralists have been heavily taxed though largely neglected in national planning. They contribute to the welfare of the urban population by providing meat and direct and indirect taxes. Camels are seen as a source of foreign exchange through the export of camels in Middle East, as a beast of burden for transporting crops, especially cotton, from farm to market and as a source of hides and also of meat when beef prices are beyond the incomes of poor urban dwellers. This leads us to a closer look at the contribution of camels to the Sudanese economy in general and to food supplies (in the Sudan and the Middle East) in particular.

CAMEL PRODUCTION AS FOOD AND FOREIGN EXCHANGE EARNER: THE
NATIONAL SCENE

The total population of the Sudan is about 22 millions (1983 Population
Census) and pastoralists represents about 14.3 per cent (2.91 millions). It is
also estimated that there were 49.01 million head of livestock in the country in 1985, mainly cattle, sheep, cattle and camels, which represent 5.53
per cent of the total. (Table 1)

The present picture of camel distribution in the Sudan can be seen from
Table 2 which reveals that 36.14 per cent of the camel population is in
Kordofan region, 28.09 per cent in the Eastern region, 15.59 per cent in
Darfur region, 11.12 per cent in the Central region, 7.07 per cent in the
Northern region and 1.41 per cent in the wetter zone in the Southern regions. The existence of large numbers of camel herds in the Southern regions is associated with the last drought, which is a new factor for camel
pastoralists in the Sudan. It also implies that new systems of adaptation are
emerging which require further research on the response of camels to life
in the new ecological zone to which they have been moved.

The *abala* or camel pastoralists represent about 750 000 inhabitants or 3.4
per cent of the total population of the Sudan. This estimate is derived from
the 1956 Population Census, the only census that classifies the population
according to ethnic group. The estimates give an average holding of 2.92
(or 3) camels per person. Considering that the average household size in
rural Kordofan is 7 members, it follows that the average household holding can be estimated at 21 camels. Although such statistical data is mean-
ingless in terms of differentiation between rich and poor households, it ties
very well with Asad (1970), who estimates that a household requires an
optimum herd size of 20 female and male camels to be economically viable
in pursuing nomadic life.

Sudan's total consumption of red meat in 1983 was 7.7 million animals.
Camels represent 8.8 per cent of the animals slaughtered in official slaughterhouses but 18 to 20 per cent of the total meat consumed per annum due
to their large size. The 1985 Economic Survey estimated that camels provided 33 657 metric tons of meat, leaving a surplus of 40, 000 camels for
export (of a value of about USD 30 million according to the official exchange rate). This is shown as follows:

Annual Meat Offtake 1985/86
(in metric tons)

Livestock	Cattle	Goats	Sheep	Camels
Offtake	423 963	68 028	48 251	33 657

Source: Economic and Social Research Council, 1987

Livestock contributed 40.5 million dollars in foreign exchange earnings with exports to the Middle Eastern countries. According to official statistics from the Ministry of Commerce, camels contributed 6.7 per cent of total export income and accounted for 25 per cent of foreign exchange earned from livestock exports. These figures exclude smuggling to Egypt and Libya across the Sahara.

Despite a substantial contribution to the national economy and food supply, livestock received less than 0.94 per cent of the financial resources allocated under the Six Year plan 1980/81-1985/86 and have inadequate health and water supply facilities. According to the 1985 Economic Survey there were 55 veterinary health centres, 58 veterinary hospitals and 238 small dressing stations, all poorly equipped. The water situation is even worse. The 1986/87 Report of the National Water Corporation (NWC) revealed that between 35 to 46 per cent of the bore holes are not functioning due to lack of spare parts and fuel shortage. The same Report reveals that about 50 per cent of the reservoirs are silted up due to lack of maintenance and long periods without rain. The marginal lands where, camels are grazed lack even these poor facilities and herdsmen are dependent on the more reliable but fatiguing traditional system of drawing water from wells and buying high-priced medicines form the black market of the Government stores.

Looking at this grim picture one can argue that adequate water supplies and health services are prerequisites for a balanced production of camels and camel products. At present pastoralists, like other producers of primary products, finance the very system that consciously attempts to squeeze more pennies from them.

Camel pastoralism is seen as a production system which can yield foreign exchange earnings with or without any expenditure on the part of the government. The potential has been geared towards 1. securing meat supply to the urban dwellers and 2. increasing exports and hence foreign exchange earnings. However, these objectives were not matched by a policy of increasing productivity, eliminating constraints on production and waste of resources.

THE RESPONSE OF CAMEL PASTORALISTS TO DROUGHT AND GRAIN SHORTAGES: THE LOCAL SCENE

The impact of the 1983-85 drought on camel pastoralists in the Sudan will have more far-reaching effects than the literature so far indicates. Camel pastoralists are highly mobile and that their mobility is largely determined by the climate and the availability of food for their animals. Their environment is characterized by low rainfall, sparse vegetation and, recently, recurring natural calamities.

The ability of pastoral household to raise an optimum number of camels depends also on labour availability. The common practice is to split the household into young male herders and the rest of the family (adults, elders and children). The young able-bodied males are responsible for the tough herding activities, well-digging, watering and guarding the herd. The rest of the household look after the small animals, (usually sheep and goats) and tend the farms (if the rains are sufficient for growing grain).

Limited grain production is essential for at least two reasons: first, households usually reduce animal sales if they are able to produce sufficient grain. Second, surplus grain can be sold for cash to buy small animals or manufactured goods. Sources of income and food are diversified of risks spread.

Asad (1970) argued that the Kababish camel herders encourage families to separate so as to allow greater flexibility because they do not rely directly on camels for their food: their staple diet is millet polenta *(kisri)* served with meat. Similar arguments have also been reported by Abu Sin (1982), Salih (1985), El Tom (1987) and Holy (1987) from various camel herding communities in the Sudan.

Livestock trade, therefore, has a close relationship to grain prices. This aspect has been reported by Swift (1979), who argues that camel pastoralists in Somalia tend to lose more in terms of grain price ratios as well as of consumer goods. The subject is also treated by Hjort (1981), who suggest that the exchange rates of livestock to farm products are crucial to the standard of living of pastoralists. Farm surplus, earlier bartered with pastoralists, is now sold on the national and international markets. One effect on pastoralists is decreased availability of grain. This situation is aggravated during drought when food supplies are not readily available and have to be imported from other regions or countries. Sutter (1982) observes among the Wo Daa'be herders of Niger that the terms of trade argument is of special relevance during crisis periods such as drought when herders flood the market with weak and dying animals while millet prices are simultaneously escalating. Livestock prices usually fall while grain prices double or triple.

Table 3 shows that prices of camels were 13.3 per cent lower in 1984 than in 1983, excluding an inflation rate of about 100 per cent for the first half of 1984 and changes in real prices relative to money prices.

Table 4 gives camel prices in terms of grain prices during the peak of the drought. The value of a camel was reduced from 3.97 sacks of sorghum in 1982 before the drought to 1.60 sacks mid-1985 to the beginning of 1986. Camel producers were able to restore high prices during the end off 1986, which was a relatively good agricultural year - up to 7.53 sacks of sorghum for a medium-size camel.

A prolonged period of drought also affects the herd reproduction rate, due to heavy offtake and a high mortality rate, in most cases not compensated by new births. The 1987 Statistical Survey of the Animal Resources Economic Administration reveals that the annual growth rate of camel herds decreased from +2 per cent per annum before the drought in 1982 to the negative growth rate of -3.23 in 1985. This figure slightly recovered in 1986 to -0.28 per cent per annum.

Some households have small numbers of camels which cannot sustain them. They will allocate labour to other income-earning activities such as labouring, wood and charcoal selling, well-digging and crafts such as rope and leather work. In Sudan many rural families have migrated to the towns. The Regional Planning Unit of Kordofan Region reported that 35-40 per cent of impoverished Kababish (elderly, women and children) migrated to towns such as El Obeid and Omdurman during the 1983-85 drought. The same applies to the Beja, who have depopulated the Red Sea Hills by about 50 per cent since 1972 and now live either as destitutes in Port Sudan, Kassala or work as seasonal agricultural labourers in the Gash and Toker Delta Schemes.

During my fieldwork in North Kordofan and Northwest Omdurm District, some households reported that they were short of labour due to the migration of youngsters to towns. This has three negative effects:

1. Water is obtained from wells 40-60 m deep that require continuous maintenance. This job is traditionally done by youngsters, but if they leave it has to be done by elderly men and the women who are left behind. As their food reserves dry up and their bodies become weaker they were finally unable to do the work.
2. Some households were not able to migrate with the herd to the wetter southern zone where browsing trees were still available and water obtainable from shallow, hand-dug wells. This fact was coupled with the problems of the psychology of hunger, which separates rather than brings people together and led to the breakdown of the traditional solidarity and sharing at a time when there was very little to share.

3. Camel pastoralism is practised in low-populated areas, with very limited marketing opportunities. The main camel markets of Omdurman, Dongola, Umm Badir, El Fashir, Tambool, Kassala, El Obeid, Melleit and others are all located in urban centres hundreds of miles away. The camel trade involves long journeys, usually carried out by young men during the rainy season. However, during periods of drought the labour-intensive herding and watering activities are carried out through the year. If they could not get their animals to market, the camel herdsmen would resort to middlemen and speculators, who usually offer very low prices, in order to finance grain and other food purchases.

When the pastoral system was on the verge of total collapse, camel pastoralists resorted to their traditional knowledge to obtain food from wild plants. El Tom (1987) observes among the Zaghawa, the Berti and the Messalit of Northern Darfur that they used Haskanit (Cenchrus biflrus) as a substitute for millet, also treated the Mukheit (Bosica Sengalensis) and Koreib (Panicum Laetum) and mixed them with millet to make porridge or local beer *(marisa)*. El Tom argues that use of the wild plants indicates the frequency of crop failures in the area. As demand for these wild plants increased their prices also increased tremendously.

As all available sources of food gradually become exhausted, some migrate to towns while others who are left with small numbers of animals begin to practice sedentary pastoralism. The case of the Kababish, Guriyat, the Ahamda and Kawahla, who migrated to Northwest Omdurman, illustrates this emerging pastoral way of life. I observed (1985) in the northwest of Omdurman that sedentary pastoralism was being practised, and camel milk and clarified butter sold in Omdurman market. Camels are also used for transporting firewood and charcoal to town and returning with water and other essentials.

The next question is what policy issues are of prime importance in order to achieve a balanced system of food production for camel pastoralists.

BRIDGING THE PERCEPTION GAP: A SYNTHESIS OF THE NATIONAL AND THE LOCAL SCENE

Simpson (1984) argues that, while the Government has a vested interest in increasing productivity and reducing the retail cost of meat and associated products, individual producers do not share these objectives or, if they do, only marginally as their major interest lies in the welfare of their families.

Herders' associations are needed as a vehicle for consciousness raising and also for the following reasons:

a) to allocate the real control over rangelands and pastoral water sources to the traditional pastoral users. In the arid lands, when farmers are unable to earn enough from their farms they attempt to meet their needs by bringing more land under the hoe (or the tractor). (Horowitz and Little, 1987.)
b) to create institutions by which areas of range can be administered and managed communally; and,
c) to decentralize grain distribution and the provision of credit so as to allow herders to purchase grain when prices are lower, which is what pastoralists consider development projects should do for them.

Also needed are other forms of intervention such as health, water and education services. However, it is urban not rural dwellers who win out in the competition for meagre national resources.

Sørbø (1985), Kadouf and Salih (1986) and Ahmed (1987) show that the expansion of large scale mechanized schemes in the irrigated and rainfed sectors in the Sudan have attracted huge transfers of financial and technical resources at the expense of the traditional producers, both cultivators and pastoralists. Sørbø (ibid) has particularly highlighted the problem of the Shukriya camel pastoralists in the Butana of eastern Sudan. He argues that while the tenants in New Halfa irrigation scheme increasingly breed cattle, sheep and goats in different combinations, camels have become concentrated in the hands of the Shukriya, outside the scheme. While this might be expected to relieve the pressure on grazing and water resources on the Butana, the increase in the total number of livestock exerts pressures on the grazing areas, particularly as most of the *hafirs* (water reservoirs) are no longer maintained and have become of little use. These policy prejudices against camel pastoralists are reinforced by a widespread belief that camels require less attention than other domesticated species.

The present livestock policy in the Sudan is still suffering from the failure of the 1965 proposal, Project of Community Development for the Settlement of Nomads in the Sudan. The proposal was defeated by social scientists Asad, Cunnison and Hill. They maintained that settling camel pastoralists such as the Kababish would mean sacrificing the possibility of improving existing water and grazing resources and methods of rearing animals for consumption as meat. However, the present scheme with its capital intensive milk-producing village co-operatives, will cost much more, and the benefits, if realized, will be available only to a comparatively small proportion of the Kababish. Whereas Government officials think in terms of increasing the national revenue without any substantial investment, pastoralists tend to exploit the system in order to increase the productivity of their herd and so reduce the risks of their precarious way of living.

Camel production in the arid lands of the Sudan supports a large proportion of the population and contributes significantly to the national economy. As such it should be seen as an integral part of an overall policy of food security. In the case of the Sudan, it could fulfil this role if a proportion of the proceeds from the camel trade were reinvested for the welfare of the actual producers. This would require the national planning apparatus to take the side of the pastoralists and to allow the camel to bring a better standard of living to its breeders.

REFERENCES

Abu Sin, M.E. 1982: "A Change in Strategy of Animal Rearing Among the Nomads of the Butana, Eastern Sudan: A Case Study in Adaptive Response and Change in the Semi-arid Areas of the Sudan", in G. Heinsitz (ed): *Problems of Agricultural Development in the Sudan.* Esttingen.

Ahmed, A.M. (ed) 1976: *Some Aspects of Pastoral Nomadism in the Sudan.* Khartoum University Press.

Ahmed, A.M. 1987: "National Ambivalence and External Hegemony: The Negligence of Pastoralists in the Sudan", in M.A. Mohamed Salih (ed): *Agrarian Change in the Central Rainland, Sudan.* Uppsala: Scandinavian Institute of African Studies.

Asad, T. 1970: *The Kababish Arabs.* Praeger Publishers.

Asad, T., Cunnison, I. and Hill, L. 1976: "Settlement of Nomads in the Sudan: A Critique of Present Plans", in Ahmed, A.M. (ed): *Some Aspects of Pastoral Nomadism in the Sudan.* Khartoum University Press.

El Tom, A.O. 1987: "The Implications of 1980s Drought on the Rural Sahel of the Sudan", in M.A. Mohamed Salih (ed): *Agrarian Change in the Central Rainland, Sudan.* Uppsala: Scandinavian Institute of African Studies.

Hjort, A. 1981: "Herds, Trade and Grain: Pastoralism in Regional Perspective", in J.G. Galaty (ed): *The Future of Pastoral People..* Ottawa, Canada: IDRC,.

Hjort, A. June 1986: "Pastoral Life in Drylands". Input paper to SAREC Workshop on: *A Research Programme on Deforestation and Desertification.*

Horowitz, M. and Little, P.D. 1987: "African Pastoralism and Poverty: Some Implications for Drought and Famine", in M.H. Glantz (ed): *Drought and Hunger in Africa.* Cambridge University Press.

Kadouf, H. and Salih, M. 1986: *Land Tenure and Development Issues in the Rainfed Sector, Sudan.* Sudan: Ministry of Planning.

Little, P.D. 1983: "The Livestock/Grain Connection in northern Kenya: An Analysis of Pastoral Economics and Semi-arid Lands Development in Africa", in: *Rural Africana,* Vol 15/16.

Salih, M.A. Mohamed. 1985: "Pastoralists in Town: Some Recent Trends of Pastoralism in northwest Omdurman District", in: *Pastoral Network Papers,* No 21b, August.

Salih, M.A. Mohamed, 1987: "Landed Property versus Communal Rights Over Land: The Land Question in the Central Rainlands of the Sudan." A paper presented for *Bayreuth Project on African Identities.* June

Simpson, J.R. 1984: "Problems and Constraints, Goals and Policy Conflict Resolution in the Development of Sub-Saharan Africa's Livestock Industry", in J.R. Simpson and P. Evangelon (eds): *Livestock Development in Sub-Saharan Africa: Constraints, Prospects and Policy.* Westview Press.

Sørbø, G. 1985: *Tenants and Nomads in Eastern Sudan: A Study of Economic Adaptation in the New Halfa Scheme.* Uppsala: Scandinavian Institute of African Studies.
Sutter, J. 1982: "Commercial Strategies, Drought and Monetary Pressure: Wo Daa'be Nomads of Tanout Arrondissement, Niger", in: *Nomadic Peoples*, No 2.
Swift, J. 1979: "Development of Livestock Trading in Nomad Pastoral Economy: The Somali Case", in: *Pastoral Production and Society.* Cambridge University Press.
Swift, J. 1982: "The Future of African Hunter-Gatherers and Pastoral Peoples", in: *Development and Change*, 13.
Swift, J. (ed), 1984: *Pastoral Development in Central Niger.* USAID.

TABLES

Table 1. *Livestock Population in the Sudan, 1955-1985 (in millions)*

Year	Total livestock units	Camels	%	Cattle	%	Sheep	%	Goats	%
1955	35.70	2.4	6.72	12.10	33.89	11.40	31.93	9.80	27.45
1973	40.70	2.69	6.60	14.15	34.77	13.37	32.85	10.49	25.77
1977	53.52	3.00	5.60	17.89	33.42	17.24	32.24	15.59	29.13
1983	53.70	2.80	5.21	19.30	35.94	18.50	34.45	13.10	24.39
1985	49.01	2.71	5.53	17.80	36.32	15.40	31.42	13.10	26.72

Sources: 1955/1956 Census, 1976 Livestock Census, National Economic Conference, 1984, Ministry of Economic, Finance and National Planning, 1985/1986.

Table 2. *The Distribution of Camel Population in the Sudan by Region 1980-81-- 1986-87*

Region	1980-81	1981-82	1982-83	1983-84	1984-85	1985-86	1986-87
Kordofan	955,809	974,925	993,545	1,012,522	1,014,345	981,581	978,832
Eastern	743,054	753,915	772,390	787,142	788,559	763,088	760,950
Darfur	412,376	420,623	428,656	436,842	437,627	423,198	422,013
Central	293,126	296,988	340,681	310,499	311,056	301,977	301,131
Northern	187,105	190,847	194,492	198,207	198,564	192,149	191,605
Southern Regions	37,353	38,100	38,827	39,538	39,639	38,358	38,250
Khartoum	15,389	15,696	15,996	16,301	16,330	15,802	15,758
Total	2,644,212	2,691,094	2,784,587	2,801,105	2,806,120	2,716,153	2,708,539

Source: Animal Resources Economic Administration, June 1987.

Table 3. *Livestock price differences 1982-1986*

Year	Cattle			Sheep			Goats			Camels		
	price	diff.	%	price	diff.	%	price	diff.	%	price	diff.	%
1982	302	17.6	6.18	75.8	24.6	48	35	120	120	357	76	27
1983	407	104.7	34.6	140.8	64.4	85	91	56	56	455	88	24
1984	461.5	54.5	13.4	145.3	5.1	3.6	126	35	38.5	390	-65	-13.3
1985	626.6	65.1	35.7	197.3	52.0	35.7	55	-71	-26.3	479	89	22.9
1986	1,286.3	659.7	105.3	303.6	106.3	53.8	124.8	69.8	126.9	1,382	903.1	188.5

Source: Livestock and Meat Marketing Corporation, 1986/1987

Table 4. *Camel Prices Measured in Sorghum Prices 1982-1986*

Year	Camel prices per unit of 450 kg	Sorghum prices per sack of 100 kg	Sacks of Sorghum per camel
1982	LS 357	LS 90	3.97
1983	455	150	3.03
1984	390	240	1.63
1985	479	300	1.60
1986	903.1	120	7.53

Source: Price Index: Department of Statistics, 1987. Livestock and Meat Marketing Corporation, 1986/1987.

Sustainable Subsistence in Arid Lands; The Case of Camel Rearing

Anders Hjort af Ornäs

Many people in the third world live today at a minimum level of subsistence. One thing they have in common is their vulnerability. They have, or consider that they have, few alternatives to their current situation. The seem to others as desperate people who do not have the opportunity to respect ecological balance, economic laws, social justice or political democracy. Immediate problems of survival have to be solved first; a long-term perspective with balanced agricultural systems is not seen as a relevant issue in the perspective of poor people.

This is one way in which poor people are considered in today's debate on environmental problems and development: land is degraded and trees cut by people who do not consider long-term negative effects.

It is however possible to shift perspective and include the situation and viewpoint of the vulnerable person. We will then speak about the security of the individual instead of national and international security problems. With this shift the following questions might arise: What kind of resources are available to the individual? How do natural resources link with others assets for the individual, such as contact networks, access to information, know-how etc? With this change in perspective we might reach beyond a descriptive analysis of the present and gain deeper insights into why imbalances occur. Land degradation then becomes a symptom of deeper causes rather than a problem in itself.

It would then be easier and more meaningful to try to give meaning to the notion of sustainable systems.

Research attention has recently focussed on arid lands, but the camel and camel rearing are still under-researched. This is true not only for social and economic aspects but also the veterinary aspects.

The camel is ecologically of great interest. It is extremely well-suited for a life in arid lands. It can suffer hot climates and move longer without water than any other domestic animal. It has big soft feet which do not destroy the vegetation. Furthermore, it provides milk almost all year around in great quantities that has a high nutritional quality. It is resistant to disease.

Camel herding, however, is changing drastically. A permanent migration of young people to the towns and cities has rendered livestock rearing less efficient in many countries due to an acute shortage of labour. What new forms we may see for the future is a basic question for researchers to answer.

General tendencies and problems within subsistence systems

Production systems based on camel rearing have a great potential for certain regions. This fact and the quickly growing interest in camels within the international development community also holds a potential danger. If initiatives from the outside come before an insight into the often intricate ways in which camel pastoralism operates, the danger is great for some kind of uncontrolled development. Therefore there is an acute need for research that links closely with development plans. Great attention must be given to existing production systems where the camel is included in order to identify weak points in the system. Conclusions should be drawn on two levels: what kind of support can be given to existing systems, and how alternatives that do not risk destroying these systems can be formulated.

A first step is therefore to identify characteristic traits of camel pastoralism that hold a potential or hide a weakness.

Reproduction of family herds and society
The growth rate in a family herd of camels is low due to biological and ecological conditions. The camel is considerably more resistant to drought than other domestic animals. In a subsistence economy we may regard the camel herd as a fairly constant resource, with a not too dissimilar role to that of the field for the farmer.

Yet production capacity, the reproduction of the family herd, and hence to some extent also the reproduction of the entire community, are continuously threatened. As a result of the high risks linked with the regrowth of herds, the camel keeper must pay much attention to his turn-over of capital in the form of animals. Herd management has to consider both immediate food production requirements and long-term capital care aspects, such as reproduction. Cultural systems often emphasize this fact through social pressure against uncontrolled sale of animals.

Management and work
The labour needed for management of family camel herds varies seasonally. There are different camel breeds and great fluctuations in the quality of pasture. Hence one finds variations in migration patterns, albeit to a large extent either highly nomadic or fairly settled. Furthermore, great variations in access to water (dams, deep wells, etc) and climatic differ-

ences between areas with one or two rainy seasons influence labour requirements.

Diversification of livestock management

Large and already sustainable households have the capacity to diversify management and keep various domestic animals. This is a way of spreading risks. There is a tendency for transition from camel to small stock rearing when marketing is improved. A general stratification of camel herding communities also seems to occur at present; viable camel herds are managed by fewer but wealthier persons than in the past. One might forecast a change from intensive livestock keeping focussing on milk and meat production from family herds to more extensive methods, where production is more geared towards marketing of live animals. If this is the case we will in future witness a limited number of owners who control great numbers of camels.

Production for subsistence

Family herds of camels give milk but also meat, hump fat , wool and hides. Production data and detailed data on herd structures are still rare. It is clear that milk output is high, considering the ecological circumstances. The nutritional value of milk is great. Even if the taste is different from other milk, its potential contribution to food production in arid lands deserves great attention. Hides also deserve attention, not least since the leather is exceptionally strong.

Marketing

Marketing of live animals is an important trade, especially in countries with a large camel population. The general price level has increased substantially resulting in the depletion of many regional herds. Also, females are at times traded in spite of the fact that most countries have a ban on their export.

Transport and power

The total number of people specializing in camel rearing is probably not particularly great. In comparison, the number of persons depending on camels for transport is far greater. It might even be that the camel's greatest single importance is for short distance transport and as draught animals in farming. But no precise data are available: being neither manufactured or imported, the camel does not figure in national statistics. Only in times of crisis, e.g. when short distance transportation fails due to too few camels or donkeys, does the importance show.

The topics listed above have been dealt with at workshops dealing with camel pastoralism in a unique setting where herdsmen and scholars meet. So far these have been arranged in Kenya, Mali and Somalia. Discussions have been intense between the two categories of participants. Topics discussed have included very specific issues, (e.g. veterinary ones); as well as conditions necessary for camel pastoralism to survive. One observes a rapid change in ownership structure, and a general tendency for camel rearing to become more specialized and market oriented, while camel herding as a way of life is changing.

Key issues for future camel pastoralism

Expectations on development inputs are very different depending on whether the minister, the planner, the administrator, the local politician or the ordinary man speaks. A concensus does not exist beyond a rhetorical level. Projects are planned from the outside and based on only partial local information. Normally, better information is needed on the planners' side. There is a very small margin between survival and disaster, so failures can not really be permitted. The situation prohibits a trial-and-error kind of approach.

The basic problems when we seek a "deeper insight" can in actual fact be said to fall into four categories: (1) difficulties to uphold a really long-term perspective; and (2) problems on the planning and administrative side; (3) a lack of basic data; and (4) an often hostile attitude from a population which has already been "bombarded" by development aid of poor quality.

One dilemma is of course the conflict between different interests on the one hand those of an urban population, on the other hand the interests of herdsmen or farmers, usually belonging to an ethnic minority. One "minimal" rule-of-thumb could be that nobody should be worse off due to a development project. This sounds strange but against the background of partial failure of several large-scale development projects it becomes almost like a political demand from poor people. The most common kind of "unplanned development" is when new land-use techniques are introduced and new groups resettled, such as when herdsmen find great difficulties to get access to reserve grazing areas or river beds for water.

How, then, can local perspectives be respected? The following issues are among those of great importance:

1. To see the family herd as the basic economic production unit. Though it does not show up in commercial and trade data, it is fundamental for

the livelihood of camel herders and their families. Without their herds they will migrate to the city slums. The herd and not the land is the prime resource.

2. In order to comprehend living conditions we must understand the conditions for herd management, such as:
   - herd "demography" (including a striving to reach an even age distribution within the herd)
   - disaster effects
   - pre- and post-drought situations
   - dry and milk herds
   - choices of different species.

3. The dilemma of private herds and common lands has to be considered. It links with the issue of alternative land-use practices, not least agropastoralism (combining farming and animal husbandry).

4. Greater attention must be given to how the animals are reared and the land managed. A camel herd might be seen as a constant asset with a given food output, in this respect not dissimilar to a farm. This means that cattle and camel herding are very different kinds of undertaking although they are two aspects of pastoralism. An interesting development of late (e.g. among the Samburu of Kenya) is that people change from cattle rearing to camels. Such a change is profound, and goes at times against established value systems; it means new forms of production, new know-how, new labour demands, different seasonal dependencies, changes in social life.

5. Seasonal fluctuations are complex but important to comprehend in detail. The carrying capacity varies dramatically, as do milk production and labour requirements.

6. There are many "symbiotic" relations between different production forms. One must master the whole system even if parts of it lie outside the arid lands. There are examples of how disturbances lead to understocking (Borana/Sakuye in Kenya).

7. Respect for existing knowledge. The "outside world" has a contribution to make to the local community but it tends to dominate and leave local voices unheard.

This list of considerations is both brief and incomplete. It has been discussed in greater detail elsewhere (cf. Dahl and Hjort 1976 and 1979). But it should be comprehensive enough to demonstrate the foundations for decision-making among the inhabitants of arid lands, members of the target group with which the industrialized world expresses its solidarity through development aid. Without comprehending actual life situations we shall never be able to forecast scenarios for the future except in the overall time perspective that is offered by the study of climatic changes. And a first step is to fill such gaps of knowledge as I have just indicated.

Let us depart from a most fundamental ecological model in order to approach some of these gaps:

Figure 1. *Simplified people/land/livestock relationship*

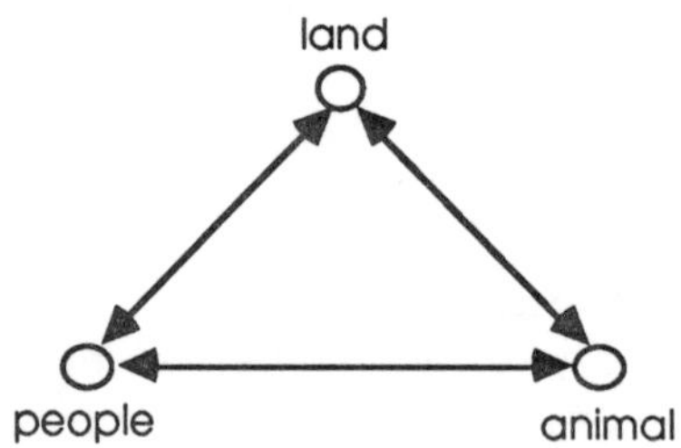

a) *Animals:* What is generally studied is numbers and types of animals, production figures of the individual animal, possibly their fodder demand and average herd sizes on a regional basis. Also central for a systematic understanding are: (1) age structures and "demographic" studies (a division into calves, immature and mature animals); (2) a food production perspective using the family herd as the production unit; (3) a search for how <u>a household</u> combines different animals, farming and not least urban or semi-urban activities (about one third of the inhabitants in the rural areas may find their living from other means than herding or farming); (4) seasonality in milk output.
b) *Land* is a scarce resource. Nevertheless what is generally studied is the carrying capacity of the land. Aspects that are often neglected include: (1) the detailed inventory of which local plants are suitable for which species of livestock; (2) seasonal fluctuations; (3) capacity of different plants to serve as emergency fodder; (4) alternative capacities of land (e.g. extensive farming versus high quality livestock rearing); (5) land ownership and the issue of effective control and hence proper land management.
c) *People:* Here we find demographic studies with growth rates, mortality, fertility, etc. What are to a considerable extent lacking are the societal and cultural dimensions: (1) Traditional know-how; (2) Herd management; (3) Security dimensions; (4) Political and other conflicts. Also much more must be understood of *decision-making* and *competence.*

Security requirements of the household are basic to an understanding of living conditions:

- Many children are needed in order to achieve a secure position;

- Many animals are required to keep starvation at bay;
- Social networks give a security by offering various forms of solidarity (see Hjort, 1979, for a presentation of four different insurance principles).

So much for some of the more important issues concerning the individual components. Let us now look at how they relate:

d) *Land and animals:* The relationship often involves statistical terms such as land's average (sic) carrying capacity or stock units. Sometimes lip service is paid to the fact that variations are so great that averages disguise the situation, or to the fact that domestic animals have selective grazing and browsing habits. But rarely is "the worst case" utilized in connection with carrying capacity, or a differentiation made between different species when it comes to utilization of pastures. These are needed corrections, and they are in line with the need to obtain more of a local perspective in order to comprehend the actual living situations: Decision making must often be based on the worst case in order to maintain a margin to disaster. Decisions concerning family herds are made from viable combinations of livestock species, not of stock units.

e) *People and animals:* This relation is usually discussed in carrying capacity terms, i.e. herds' capacity to provide food for people. What are often lacking are considerations of work inputs (except for aggregated data). Seasonality in work requirements and a combined consumption/production analysis is required. Figure 2 illustrates how more pertinent information can be obtained. The graph demonstrates how a series of viable people/animals combinations may exist, not just one optimal combination. There is more information in this kind of systemic conclusion than in one based on aggregate information. It opens the door for consideration of decision-making, competence and herding techniques.

From this long list of important issues for the future of camel pastoralism one might single out four for a consideration of development options:

1. Age structures and 'demographic' studies. What is available is normally only a division into calves, immatures and mature animals);
2. A food production perspective using the family herd as the production unit;
3. A search for how a household combines different domestic animals, farming, and urban or semi-urban activities.
4. Seasonality in milk output.

Figure 2. *Correlation between numbers of animals and people in consumption and production perspectives*

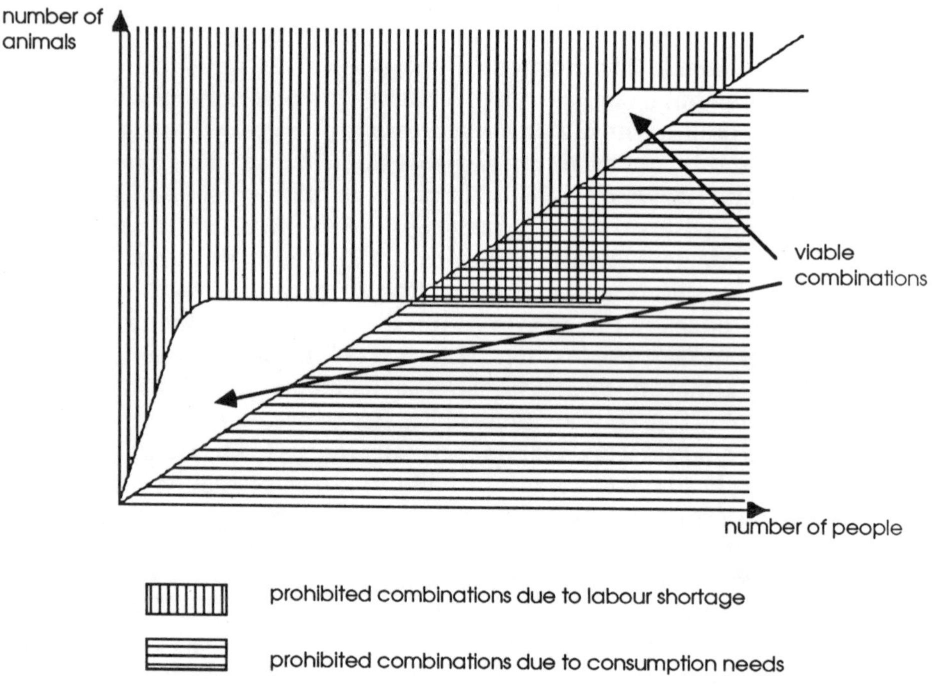

Some special tendencies pertaining to today's extensive livestock rearing

Basic to the rapid change in living conditions is the problem of high human and animal population pressure. Ecological factors would seem to influence the conditions for each individual, as well as a wealth of political, cultural and economic. All in all the situation of inequality seems to be created or maintained. This, however, could be brought to an end if we were to gain deepened insights into factual circumstances. I would like to illustrate this with five examples which concern how land is utilized. They are selected in order to illustrate different tendencies for change, situations where conditions seem to be deteriorating and those that are promising.

1. *High risk rainfed farming versus high quality camel rearing in Northeastern Sudan*. This is a case of land rights on a kin-group basis, with the implication that land is a collective resource. No fundamental conflict arises

as long as everyone deals with camel rearing. But a drought disaster led to the extinction of entire family herds. The impoverished families then began farming on the collective land a situation of poor quality farms ruining high quality pastures.

2. *Pastoralists and agropastoralists competing in Northern Kenya*. People in the same area have two different goals with their livestock rearing. One group depends on milk and needs better pastures than the other, which invests its farming profits in non-milk-producing cattle.

3. New production systems alongside extensive livestock rearing (cow/calf systems; bank systems; dairy production). Cow/calf systems with back-feeding in arid lands of immatures are at times included in development projects. In the pastoralist's perspective, the work investment is with the cow/calf and keeping immatures is practically no extra work. In the same perspective, back-feeding means control over the animals is lost, in that they are kept on land outside one's "own" territory. Bank system implies de-stocking through a livestock bank system. For the pastoralist this is a good idea granted that the bank is under proper control. Dairy production is viable if the milk used is really surplus. Somalia, where milk is collected seasonally, provides an interesting case. Local control might open up new avenues to modifications in land use.

4. *The Lake Turkana fishing project*. This illustrates how cash can be fed into a subsistence-based production system. Money earned outside pastoralism is invested in a pastoral economy by means of improved health (veterinary medicine) and purchasing instead of exchanging livestock. The flow of resources may change with an uncontrolled development so that entire production systems are knocked out of balance.

5. *The Samburu shift from cattle to camel rearing*. In this case the focus is a "spontaneous" development caused by people's ecological observations and desire to achieve a balanced and reliable situation. As already mentioned, this signifies a shift from cattle to camels in an extremely cattle-oriented section of the population, implying fundamental change (such as learning new techniques and reorganizing social life). New ways of utilization of dryland areas can clearly be conceived of if we are to generalize from this example.

One all-important question when it comes to conflicting use of dryland areas is to what degree our prime concern has to be to stop starvation and improve the quality of life, and to what degree it is to halt land degradation. Obviously both are worthy goals. Social scientists have a contribution to make here by showing how resources are inter-woven into systems of land use on a grassroot level. Ecologists who concentrate on land management systems could be in a position not only to analyse current situations but also to decode warning signals about threats against a natural resource base. Obviously, both long-term and detailed empirical projects are needed. This goes not only for natural resources but also for demographic information, since the latter is so often used to explain current situations. We need to understand the foundations for decision-making when it comes to the use of dryland areas. Without it we shall never be able to design scenarios for the future.

DISCUSSANT'S REPORT

Moses O. Awogbade

Three papers were presented during the first session, each dealing with issues of camel pastoralism.

While the papers by Mustafa and Salih dealing with the Sudan are localized, the paper from Hjort takes a critical look at the political economy informing various development strategies of camel rearing in drylands Africa. He calls for a holistic approach to livestock development.

A run-down of the papers will help to identify some of the fundamental issues and provide material for further discussion.

An appeal for a modified camel productivity

A case is made for the unrivalled productivity of the camel and its potential for adaptation to the African drylands. The paper deals with the role of the camel in socio-political, economic and cultural life of the people in the Arabian peninsula. From this historical perspective the focus changes to the present situation in the Sudan. Of particular interest are issues dealing with camel population, the ecological components that influence production and herd displacement.

Professor Mustafa is concerned mainly with how to modify existing cultural practices by camel pastoralists with a view to increasing productivity and improving the livelihood of herd owners. At the same time, he cautions about disturbing the social life of the nomads. But I believe the question to be asked is simply this: Is it possible to reach the desired goal in pastoral development without tampering with an age-old tradition? If the answer is yes, then the question is: what is to be modified? (Migratory tendency? Production system? Marketing system?)

The fundamental issue is the direction that development must take so as to achieve a balanced food system for both humans and animals.

In conclusion, the paper suggests five ways that a modified camel productivity could be achieved. The first two suggestions seem to be attainable. The others (3-5), although laudable, are bound to create both financial and logistical problems for the Sudanese government. This is a personal view, open to modification.

Camel Production in the Arid Lands of the Sudan: National and Local Perception of the Potential

The focus of Dr Salih's paper, is on how to achieve a balanced food system in the Sudan sub-region. Two irreconcilable perceptions are identified: that of planners on the viability of projects and their potential for recovering costs; and that of technicians concerned with achievement of balanced production in the arid lands of the Sudan.

Two possible effects of this clash of perceptions are identified: (a) dependency and loss of control over commercialization of pastoral production; (b) widening of the development gap between pastoralists and sedentarists (who, incidentally, have been enjoying relatively better social and medical services at the expense of pastoralists).

A way out of this inequality of access to social services is to create *contact points* where the views of those most vulnerable to natural calamities can be understood and ameliorated. Examples in Sudan are given to support this concept. Of importance here are the (a) livestock/grain exchange relationship and (b) the unfavourable position of pastoralists in the international market.

Economic exploitation of the pastoralists by the government is aptly described: "the national perception of camel pastoralism is that it is a source of foreign exchange...". The paper then takes a look at the camel's contribution to the Sudanese economy. Dr Salih is highly critical of government policy on livestock production, and of the unequal socio-economic terms and welfare status of camel pastoralists.

Sustainable Subsistence in Arid Lands: The Case of Camel Rearing

According to Anders Hjort, "many people in the Third World population today experience a living at a level of minimum existence". The question of their survival, he argues, is what must be solved first. Therefore, the social and political dimension of development takes precedence. There is a need "to shift emphasis from international security to individual security" and to develop projects with an environmental dimension that concern the very foundation of man's existence: land, water, vegetation, livestock etc.

It is in this context that the paper starts to deal with arid lands and the development of camel pastoralism. Hjort then takes a brief look at the growing interest in camel rearing within the international development communities. But he calls for thorough understanding of the intricate ways camel pastoralism operates before any development interventions are made. Greater attention must be given to the existing production system so as to identify its strong and weak points.

Two important areas which I believe could be discussed extensively are:

1) What kind of support should be given to the existing system; and
2) how to formulate alternatives that do not risk breaking down what already exists.

The paper is mindful of the inherent conflicts between local and national interests, although their nature is not discussed. I believe further discussion can be profitable when one understands the background of these conflicts and can relate it to the whole question of sustainable subsistence in its theoretical and practical dimensions.

Hjort's idea of the responsibility of social scientists should not go unnoticed (see p 10). I also believe he is mindful of the conflict of interest between national goals and the scientists' narrow specialized concerns. Maybe we should discuss this aspect, too.

Pastoral systems at Loggerheads

Ayele Gebre Mariam

The Arsi and the Somali pastoralists inhabit southern Bale and particularly Dello Awraja and Meda Welabu districts. This article[1] is concerned with external factors that cause the impoverishment of the Arsi and Somali, who live in absolute poverty, despite the fact that camels can survive periods of stress. Ecological factors do not lead to degradation of the rangelands but are triggered off by political factors.[2] Before analyzing the political factors that lead to their impoverishment, I will show how they adapt to the ecological environment.

ECOLOGICAL ADAPTATION

The subsistence economy of the Arsi and Somali does not depend on camels alone; however, issues resulting of the rearing of other species such as cattle, goats and sheep are not dealt with here.
The different breeds of camels include:

horka	big size, with no or very little hair. It is mostly owned by the Digodia.
geleb	medium size, hardy and drought resistant beast.
gebiro or *hedimo*	dark skinned and hairy. This breed of camel was brought to Meda Welabu from Gabbra territory in 1940.

These different camel breeds have different comparative advantages. *Horka* is selected for milk and meat and is a less hardy animal. *Geleb* is a

---

[1] This article is based on field research in southern Bale, Dello Awraja and Meda Welabu district from February 1987 to September 1987. The material was collected while carrying out a social anthropological study for Norwegian Church Aid (NCA). I am indebted to NCA, which gave me valuable assistance. I am particularly grateful for comments by Mohamed Salih as well as the workshop participants. My travel tickets and attendance at the workshop were paid by SIAS and I wish to express my gratitude for this.

[2] See Dahl, G. 1979: *Suffering Grass: Subsistence and Society of the Isiolo Boran.* Stockholm: Stockholm Studies in Social Anthropology, Department of Social Anthropology.

drought-resistant beast, but its milk and meat yield is less than that of *horka*. *Gebiro* is smaller in size than the *Geleb* but gives more milk.

Camels feed on different shrubs and bushes[1] in different seasons. Some bushes and shrubs are mainly used in the dry, wet or drought periods and others in only one of these periods. Forage species of value to camels in the dry season include *shekoru, lekume, biresa, hameresa, sidamo, megega, galo, measa, jirme, hada, hagerso, besduga, sare debo, duresoba, musduga, loketo, dumuga, kokoro, daresa, dene, muglo, ano, gora, jeldo, gongoma, lebobesa, deki, hurufo,* and *keke*.

The main wet season forages include *sare debo, duresoba, rabeley, handada, dirsoba, fursa, degire, dersoba, hagerso, besduga, kokoro, buresala, sebensa, halo, ida, dene, kursibhya, borera,* and *hameresa*.

The emergency fodder during drought periods includes *sheshe, kelkelcha, megega, birdesa, beka, jeldo, ano, gongoma, dodota, cheno, birleko, oda, measa, deke, selelcha, dersoba, lekeme, chila,* and *sidamo*.

A household does not depend on different animals alone. One of the productive activities the Arsi and Somali depend on is the cultivation of crops. Crops include *teff* (Eragrostis abyssinica), wheat, barley, maize, emer wheat, sorghum and fenugreek. Other crops are lentils, peas, chick peas, haricot beans and vegetables such as potatoes, garlic and sweet potatoes. *Teff* is the main cash crop.

Except for ploughing, women carry out all the cultivation processes. The farm consists of one single piece of land or, rarely, two plots, 2-3 minutes walk from each other. Each household own its crop plots but grazing land belongs to the community. The yield per hectare in quintals for maize, *teff,* wheat, barley, sorghum and emer wheat is 17.0, 5.1, 7.2, 11.7, 19.9, and 10.9 respectively. Profits from agriculture are invested in animals.

During periods of drought the Arsi and Somali eat wild roots and berries, which make a significant contribution to their diet and have helped the communities at least partly to survive the worst droughts.

Wild game also contribute to the diet, kudu and grey duiker being the more easily hunted. Others include greater kudu and Minelik's bush buck. Animals such as warthog, wild pig, porcupine and civet are not eaten.

Another income opportunity is the sale of incense from *gorore* and *werabele* trees and gum from *hankete, fulesa,* and *kumbi* (Commiphera Myrrha) trees.[2] Women and children collect incense and gum Arabic while herding animals that the head of the household brings to market for sale. As a result of this new income herdsmen have stopped selling small stock. Some households have even started building up their capital in small stock

---

[1] These local plants have been collected by the author and awaiting identification by a taxonomist.

[2] Scientific names are not known.

as a result of this new source of income. Demand for incense and gum Arabic is very high; both are exported and thus foreign exchange earners.

The Arsi and Somali, both men and women, make household utensils, milking and milk storing vessels, ropes and sacks from local materials so as to reduce their expenditure on manufactured goods.

Bee-keeping plays an important role in the local cash economy, though it depends on lowering plants, which in turn depend on rainfall. The main honey-producing areas are close to the mountains, also along the Welmal and Genale rivers.

Hunting wild game and bee-keeping are done by men, while women and children are responsible for the collection of wild roots and berries, incense and gum arabic.

Have these productive activities[1] made life better for the Arsi and Somali? No; these are only strategies they developed to cope with their problems, the real cause of which is political.

CAMEL PRODUCTION AS FOOD SYSTEMS

In the dry season, a camel is milked three times a day. The milk yield is 1 - 1.40 lit. in the morning, 0.7 - 1.4 lit. in the afternoon and 1.4 lit. in the evening. In the wet season milk yield ranges from 1.75 lit. to 3.5 lit. in the morning, 1.4 lit. to 3.5 lit. in the afternoon and evening. A camel is milked from 6 to 10 months and in few cases up to 16 months.[2]

Camel milk is drunk fresh and a woman who has given birth is given fresh milk until her child is 40 days old. Camel milk can be stored up to 7 days and is locally called *susa*. If it is kept for 40 days it is called *korur*; to keep it for such a long time, the water floating on top is removed before adding fresh milk. When camel milk is churned, four pebbles are put in the fire and placed in the milk when red . Then it is churned with a stick with branches on to produce butter. Another way of churning is to load a camel with a milk container while it grazes. When the animal returns in the evening, butter is collected. Herd owners estimate that 3.5 lit. of camel milk is turned into 0.2 lit. of butter.

A camel gives birth at 5 to 6 years of age. The parturition interval is 12 months. The life span of the female is 25-30 years and that of the male 18-25 years.

---

[1] The ecological area where I did my field work is large and extends from the forest belt of northern Bale to the rangelands where camels and goats predominate. The contribution of bee-keeping is insignificant in the rangelands.

[2] Two methods were used to estimate milk yield. The first method is through selecting sample households and asking them to estimate the milk yields of the different camels during different stages of lactation. The other method is actual measurement of milk yields of different she camels at different stages of lactation in the different season.

Another productive use of the camel as food is meat, though a camel is rarely slaughtered for household consumption. It is usually slaughtered when the animal gets old and members of an encampment get together for the feast. The hump is given first to men and then to women.

Except for blood, liver and stomach, the rest of the camel meat is eaten. Those who eat blood, liver and stomach are referred as Midgan/Bon.[1] Women do not eat a camel's heart and testicles and men do not eat the feet of a camel.

There is a practice of communal slaughter among camel herdsmen. A camel bull belonging to an individual is slaughtered in the dry season when food is in short supply. One of the guests is asked, in return, to pay back one male or female calf.

DOMESTIC USES OF CAMELS

Camel hides are vital for the Arsi and Somali households. They are used for making ropes, honey storage vessels, ornaments, prayer mats, sandals and for removing cattle dung from the kraal.

Male camels are used for long distance transport such as fetching rock salt, earth salt and grain. A female camel can be used as a baggage animal as well. Both Arsi and Somali travel by camel from Ethiopia to Somalia and Kenya. A camel can transport six huts, including household goods, children, kids and camel calves. Camel calves under 5 days old are loaded on the camel facing backwards. Other goods such as tea, clothes, refrigerators, stoves, weapons and bullets are transported by camel from Somalia and Kenya up to Oborsu, Angetu and even further to Gedeb. The return trip is made with coffee, grain, sugar, skins, hides, etc.

A *Horka* camel carries 3 qls of grain from Negelle to Meda and Meda to Negelle with three breaks on the way (a distance of about 240 kms) and can also carry up to 300 litres of water.

Camel butter is used for smearing the herder's hair. It is also used for frying meat and for roasting coffee *(bune kella)*.

A milking she camel is exchanged for 30 to 40 goats or 4 to 5 cows, while one immature female camel calf is exchanged for 10 qls of maize.

HERD MANAGEMENT

The Arsi and Somali have developed special skills in herd management. The camel herds are divided into home *(werra)* and dry *(ureni)*. As a result

---

[1] A Somali term for despised groups.

of drought factors and uprisings in Bale, the number of *ureni* owners have diminished in size.

Large herdowners employ four herdsmen. The camel herds are divided into the following categories:

a) bulls (kept separately, only one bull going with the females);
b) milking camels;
c) pregnant and non milking females; and
d) calves.

Those without herdsmen get relatives to herd for them and they receive one heifer camel for one year of herding. This practice is declining, however, as herds have been dwindling, due to political conflicts.

Another way of solving labour shortages is by marrying more than one wife to herd the animals.

By mixing cattle, camel and goats, for example, households obtain milk, meat and other products throughout the year. The feed requirements of each species varies, however, and cattle and sheep are more affected by stress conditions than goats and camels. This has been thoroughly discussed by Dahl and Hjort, 1976.[1]

The age and sex structure varies enormously among camels compared with other species. However, the greater proportion of the camel population consists of females. Those over 10 years of age and below one year of age are in the majority. (See Table 1.)

Another aspect of herd management is dispersion. Camels are moved to different grazing areas in different seasons. The common pattern is as follows:

rainy season	Bole
dry season	Tullu Deve
small rains	Kersa Dula
big dry season	Meda

Different species are kept with different wives. One wife may tend camels, another cattle and a third sheep and goats. Herds are dispersed for different reasons, e.g. to lessen the incidence of diseases, outbreaks of epidemics, etc. A camel's kraal has to be changed regularly, if not the animal will be disease ridden. The Arsi say "except for the hump all parts of the camel transfer diseases". Wives keep the different species in turn and thus benefiting from the different species they herd.

---

[1] Refer to Dahl, G. and Hjort, A. 1976: *Having Herds: Pastoral Herd Growth and Household Economy.* Stockholm: Stockholm Studies in Social Anthropology, Department of Social Anthropology.

Camel herds were counted at kraals, grazing areas and watering points. Breeding females, those of first parturition or more, and females in general account for 31% and 60% respectively of the total herd. This allows rapid expansion after drought or disease. A type of herd structure involving a minimum of 50% of breeding females is very suitable for assuring a continuous supply of food.

Labour demands vary between households and also according to seasonal variations in rainfall and pasture. Large herdowners need a large labour force to cater for the needs of the animals. The dry season is a time of labour shortage when drinking water for animals and humans is scarce. Because of food shortage in the dry season, household members are involved in other income generating activities. The consumption is also reduced by household members and again leads to lower efficiency in all the activities pursued. In the wet season, the opposite is true: food is available and labour demand is not so acute.

POLITICAL INFLUENCES

The political issues are factors contributing to the diminution of the livestock population, reduction in productivity, lengthening the parturition interval and increased age at first parturition. Let us look at the effect of the wars and uprisings on the Arsi and Somali communities during the last forty years.

In 1941, in what is known as the Borena war *(Woira Borena)* the Borena invaded the Arsi at Cherti on the Web river and pushed them as far as Arsi land proper. Several Arsi and Borena lost their lives. Arsi looted Borena livestock and vice-versa.

A year later, in 1942, in *Woira Captain Demessie* the Arsi moved as far as Dawa in Borena land to steal camels from Gerri. In retaliation, the government sent an army led by Captain Demessie, resulting in the death of several hundred Arsi. The war lasted two years.

The 1963-1970 Bale uprising *(dombir)* was the result of the conflict between Arsi and Somali with the Borena. The Arsi west of the Genale river were told by the governor of Borena to leave Borena Awraja and thus to cross the flooded Genale river, which then had no bridge. The Gujji also joined with the Borena to fight the Arsi and Somali. This kind of conflict has been going on because of the competition between the different economic systems over productive land. During this uprising the Ethiopian government armed the Gujji and Borena with firearms. The Arsi were armed with spears and knives, initially, until they received good quality firearms from the Somali government. Waku Gutu was the leader of the Arsi and Somali, and Colonel Defere was the commander of the

Ethiopian forces. People then used to sing that "when Wako is in Welabu and Defere is in Negelle, there is no peace".

During this uprising the Arsi lost several thousand animals. Let me show the impact of the uprising on some specimen households.

Case 1: lost 31 animals, 17 of which were slaughtered by the guerillas (the group fighting the Ethiopian government) and 14 bombarded by government planes.
Case 2: lost 100 cattle.
Case 3: lost 60 cattle, 30 camels and 100 sheep and goats and one man was killed during the uprising.
Case 4: lost 70 cattle, 80 sheep and goats and 4 camels. The military helicopter gunships killed one man and 5 of his cattle.
Case 5: lost 150 cattle to the Borena, Gujji, the army and the guerilla group.
Case 6: lost 40 cattle.

The animals were looted and killed by the Borena, Gujji and the Ethiopian government army. The guerilla group looted the animals of those Arsi and Somali who collaborated with the government and would exchange a revolver for one of their camels. The army killed some of the animals with bush knives and left them in the bush for birds and wild life. (The army used to depend on raw meat from these animals.)

The government sold several thousand animals including cattle and camels by auction in Mena and Negelle markets at minimal prices. Animal numbers have not recovered since then.

Because of the guerilla operation, livestock were moved to the forest belt in the north and because of the concentration of animals in specific area diseases were rampant. This resulted in the death of several animals.

After the uprising was over, those Arsi and Somali who fought the government for 8 years were praised and promoted in the government administration; such was the policy of Emperor Haile Selassie then. Those Arsi and Somali who were on the government side during the uprising were neglected and ignored. A similar policy was applied when Eritrea was federated with Ethiopia: those who were for federation were left out and therefore started armed struggle and those who opposed the federation were given promotion.

The *jande* uprising (1975-1981) was named after a firearm. Its cause was the rumour spread by a few Arsi and Somali that the military government, that succeeded Haile Selassie would take away their wives, children, livestock and land. Thus the Arsi and Somali again received arms from the government of Somalia and surrendered only after 8 years of struggle. During the hostilities herd owners and crop growers were forced to contribute animals and grain respectively, to the guerilla group fighting the Ethiopian troops. Several hundred animals were slaughtered. Because of the uprising, livestock were moved to the forest areas of the Bale mountains, leading to overstocking and overgrazing and resulting in lower output of food per animal (milk, meat, butter, etc).

Let me show the impact of the uprising by referring to the effect on a few households:

Case 1: lost 8 cattle, 4 camels, 15 sheep and goats to the guerilla. He also
      used to contribute 40 Birr per month to the guerilla.
Case 2: lost 5 cattle.
Case 3: lost 60 cattle.
Case 4: lost 50 cattle.

Life for the Arsi and Somali has been disrupted for 16 years due to the uprisings. For centuries political factors and conflicts with neighbouring groups and with the state have reduced the human and animal population.

The Arsi and Somali have lived on the periphery of the modernization process for several centuries. The government seems to have marginal control over their territory and they are on the fringes of the monetary economy. The potential of camel management as a food system has never been realized, for planners and administrators are alien to the pastoral communities in question.

SUMMARY AND ALTERNATIVE LAND USE

The ecological factors (land degradation, overgrazing, overstocking, etc) are not the real cause of poverty and low productivity among the Arsi and Somali; they are the symptoms rather than the cause. It is political factors (uprisings, wars) that have triggered the ecological degradation.

An alternative land use practice on the Meda Welabu rangeland may be selective breeding. I am not talking of selective breeding for camels alone, but for cattle, sheep and goats as well. The best East African breeds of livestock for meat, milk, butter, etc, are found on the belt running north of Ramo, Mandera and Moyale (Kenya side) and south of Meda, Negelle and west of Cherti (Ethiopia side). The best breeds of camels, cattle, goats and sheep are locally referred as *hor*, *dewara*, *areadi*, and *ida*, respectively. The local markets for them are situated at Negelle, Filtu, Moyale, Geddei, Ramo and Luk (in Somalia Republic). The major ethnic group in this belt include Gurra, Ajuran, Hawiya, Kerneley, Digodia, Merrihan, Bedisle, Dewed, Gerri, Geljale (in Kenya), Murle (in Kenya) and Sheikale (in Somalia).

A productivity improvement for the highland and sub-highland livestock species of Ethiopia may be through cross-breeding female an-

imals of the best breeds with imported bulls, rams and bucks for distribution to the highland farmers on a credit basis.

TABLE

Table 1. *Age Structure (camels belonging to 10 households)*

Age in Years	M	%	F	%	Total	%
0-1	11	22.4	7	9.6	18	14.8
1-2	6	12.2	3	4.1	9	7.4
2-3	7	14.3	9	12.3	16	13.1
3-4	8	16.3	8	11.0	16	13.1
4-5	2	4.1	4	5.5	6	4.9
5-6	2	4.1	4	5.5	6	4.9
6-7	2	4.1	4	5.5	6	4.9
7-8	2	4.1	2	2.7	4	3.3
8-9	-	-	7	9.6	7	5.7
9-10	2	4.1	6	8.2	8	6.6
10+	7	14.3	19	26.0	26	21.3
TOTAL	49	100.0	73	100.0	122	100.0

Camel Herding and Its Effect on Somali Literature

Mohamed Abdillahi Rirash

CAMELS: GEOGRAPHICAL REGIONS

In an arid region, like the one inhabited by the Somalis and the Afars in the Horn of Africa, camels are the dominant livestock since they are best suited to the environment. Both water *(biyo)* and pasture *(baad)* are scanty. On the average, temperatures are high throughout the year, especially along the coast.

Camels are herded in three geographical regions in this area: the *oogo*, or high plateau, the mountainous region, and the *guban*, the burnt region of the coastal strip. The first region, the *oogo*, includes a great part of the Ogaden; the other two regions are confined to the most arid parts of northern Somalia and the Republic of Djibouti.

The *oogo* region receives a relatively high rainfall during the rainy season *(gu)*. During that period, it provides the best pasture for all categories of livestock, but since it does not have permanent wells, only camels can remain there during the dry season, *jiilaal*. Then, sheep, goats and cattle are taken to areas where water is more readily available.

The type of camel that dwells in the *oogo* region is known as *caroog*. It is heavily built and has relatively thick hair *(gaameelo)* which protects it from the *oogo* chill that occurs during some stages of the *jiilaal*. The *caroog* type gives a relatively good supply of milk, but its endurance of hunger is low. For this reason *caroog* camels are kept in the waterless but pasture-rich *oogo* during the dry season. (According to my informant, the *caroog* type is very slow moving; thus, when it comes to raiding an enemy, they are very difficult to escape with.)

During the dry season in the *oogo* region, the camels are left with camel herders, the *geeljire*. These young, unmarried men make up the *geelxir*, the group that moves with the camels in isolation from the rest of the clan or the hamlet. Sometimes they do not even have a fixed settlement; they must move on, spending the night wherever they are at the end of the grazing day. (This is known as *xira daagaanle.*)

Camel herders, both the young and the grown-ups who move with the camels, carry few things with them; therefore, they, like their camels, have to dispense the water: they must depend on milk for both food and water.

From the pastureland of the *oogo*, camels are taken for watering to wells in the north. The journey to and from the wells may take several days. The *caroog* camels drink a lot of water, not to satisfy their immediate thirst, but to store it for the three or four weeks that separate watering periods *(kal)*.

For the camel herders, taking the camels for watering is both a tiring and trying business. They must endure a long walk with only a little food and camels' milk. On the way to the water wells the camels may stay overnight at different points on the road (this is known as *guulooman*: "travelling thirsty"). On the journey back to the grassland, after taking their fill, they may stay overnight at the previous points. (This time it is called *guul cokan*.) This tiring business of taking camels to and from the watering wells has been well expressed in the following song:

Geelu galabtii	Camels in the evening,
galoof iyo rimay	those which are pregnant and those which are not,
gaaniyo irmaan	those giving milk and those that are not,
isku kala gure	they sort themselves out accordingly.
anna galabtii	And, for my part in the evening,
gaajiyo harraad	in hunger and thirst,
isku kala guray	I slow up.

Although camels have a permanent settlement in the *oogo*, they make a shift into the watering region; this is called *laba xeroole*, "having two homes". In general, the *jiilaal* season is a period of instability for both the herds and the herders.

The herders who are entrusted with the care of the camels in this remote area must be well instructed in their profession. They must know where to get the *dareemo*, a grass (Chrosopogon Aucheri), that suits their camels best. Since the *caroog* type of camel does not feed on acacia trees, as is the case with other types, it must always be kept in pastureland, though the windy plains must be avoided. Wind, according to my informants, causes great discomfort for the camels; therefore, the best place to keep them is where trees make a protective shield against the winds. Herders sing this song to educate the young herders about the problems of keeping camels in windy places:

Maaru mayeybaan ku nacay	I hate the Maaro mountain because of the early
geel dabaylood baan ku nacay	morning heavy rains,
giirre jiilaalbaan ku nacayv	I hate having camels in a windy place,
	and I hate cattle when it comes to "jiilaal",
	the dry season.

An expert herder should know when to take his herds for watering, for if camels get watered before the right time *(kal)* diarrhoea may result; this is especially true when the camels are feeding on green grass. He should choose the healthiest ground for the camels in order to avoid the bites of harmful insects; the ground of his choice must be both hard and dry. He should know when to milk and when not to; in the relatively hotter areas, camels are milked only in the early morning and in the evening, but in the cooler regions, they are milked at any time during the day.

The camel herder should know when the camel is ready to be milked (*xigsin*). He should know how many of its breasts he should tie (*maraq*) and when he should tie them so they won't be suckled by the baby camels that accompany their mothers on the day's outing for grazing.

The camel herder can tie up the breasts of his she-camels in several ways. One way is to tie up either the two breasts on the lefthand side or the two breasts on the righthand side; this system is known as *xagmar*, "tying one side". The second system is known as *gayaxamar*; it consists of tying two breasts, one at the front and one at the back, but on different sides. The third method, *seddexmar*, is to tie three breasts, two in the back and one in the front.

Before feeding on grass, the breast-fed baby camel is kept in the settlement and is known as *kareeb*, "being left behind". After a period, the baby camels (*niríg*: male; *nirig*: female) go out for grazing with their mothers and the rest of the camels; when they start to feed on grass they are known as *abab*. In the first year of life baby camels (*niríg* or *nirig*) are also known as *baal cas*, "red sided" or *ilweyn*, "big eyed".

<table>
<tr><td>Bisha deyreed</td><td>In the month of Deyr</td></tr>
<tr><td>bisha dabataal</td><td>and the month that follows it,</td></tr>
<tr><td>nirig boodhliyo</td><td>you are accompanied by a brown she-camel</td></tr>
<tr><td>baal cas wadatoy</td><td>a red sided one.</td></tr>
</table>

Names of camels are given according to age or state. A baby camel or she-camel, as mentioned above, is known as *niríg* or *nirig*, depending on its sex. Around two or three years of age they are known as *qaalin* and *qaalín* respectively. Before the first calving , a she-camel is known as *ugub*; afterwards as *curad*.. A she-camel that is not impregnated though it has reached the right age is known as *abeer*. If it is neither pregnant (*rimay*) nor milking (*irman*) it is known as *galoof* and collectively as *horweyn*.. A newly calved she-camel is called *ramad*, but when it is about to stop milking it is called *gabbaan*.

On the other hand, a male camel, before it is trained as a pack animal, is known as *layli*, but after it gets used to the task it is called *raray*. A camel may be exempted from training to be kept as a stallion (*baarqab*). A *baarqab* is selected in accordance with certain qualities that are obvious from its physical appearance. From these, the camel herder can decide whether its female offspring will be *eyro*, a giver of a great amount of milk.

It is on the basis of a vast knowledge of the camel and its environment that Somali camel herders cared for the camel, bred it, and prided themselves in overcoming most of the natural difficulties that are typical of the world's arid regions. A camel herder is respected for both his endurance and his bravery; he is the vanguard of the Somali pastoralist society. As the saying goes:

Geeri nimaanad aqoon iyo geel jiray ku waansantahay. "Death is tolerable only when it comes to an unknown person or to a camel herder".

The following expresses how a camel herder sees his responsibility and how nobody can take it lightly:

Habarbaa tidhi	An old woman stated that
geelu hawl maleh	there is no hard work involved in camel herding
oo hal gudhan maleh	and here no she-camel which isn't giving milk
oo hadhaa maleh	and there is no slow-moving one within its ranks
anna waxan idhi	and I replied
hashu waxay tahay	you know nothing about a she-camel
waanad horinoo	you have never taken it for watering
waanad hoos gelin	and you never went under it to milk.

The second camel region is the mountainous area where a type of camel called *ayuun* or *cayuun* is herded. This type feeds on varieties of tall acacia trees, *geedsare laac.*

According to my informant, the *ayuun* type has a slighter build than the *caroog* type of camel. It is better suited to the rugged and more arid lands of the mountainous parts of northern Somalia and the Republic of Djibouti, but at the same time it produces less milk and is a poorer meat animal than other types.

The third camel region is the coastal strip of both northern Somalia and the Republic of Djibouti. In this region water is available but neither *oogo* pasture nor the mountain acacia grow. Therefore, the camels feed on the *xundhuun* (Suaeda Friuticosa) and *caday* (Salvadora Persica) trees which grow there in abundance. Unlike the camels in the other two regions, the coastal type does take water everyday. Though it has a lean body, it produces a greater amount of milk than the mountain type of camel. It seems that the coastal type is better adjusted to its environment, but the owners of the other two types despise it as worthless. This may be because of the small size of the herds in the coastal region.

Having discussed the environmental background to camel rearing; now let us discuss a) how the people concerned value it, and b) what effects it has on their culture and literature.

The Value of Camels

To a Somali, in general, camels mean everything. The camel is the basic unit for measuring everything he values.

Geel waa geel wixii gooyaan waa geel.
"Everything equal in value to a camel can be considered as a camel"

Though they may vary in their value, an adult she-camel is equal in value to two cows or twelve sheep. Of all the animals, only the horse has a higher value than the camel. In the western area of northern Somalia or in the Republic of Djibouti, horses are rarely used, but I am told that in certain periods, especially before the introduction of fire-arms, a horse could be exchanged for twelve camels.

The *xeer ciisa*, the customary law of the Issa, specifies that for the murder of a man, one hundred camels must be paid to the dia-paying group of the deceased; however, only seventy-seven she-camels are actually paid from one Issa clan to the other. The camels are ceremonially presented in different stages. Each and every camel must be acceptable to those who lost their clansman. The first seventeen she-camels, which are usually the best and giving milk, are presented to the relatives of the deceased; the remaining camels are evenly distributed among the dia-paying group. This privilege is restricted to the Issa clans; in other clans the camels paid as blood money are not the best. In some cases each member of the dia-paying group who is to pay the blood money presents the poorest of his she-camels; hence the expression *geel mag* (blood camels) is used to say that something is of a poor quality.

A woman's dia, which among the Issa is half that of a man, is paid in livestock other than camels; however, the number of cows or sheep should be equal in value to the number of fifty camels specified by the *xeer*. One of my informants told me that since dowry, *dhaban* (literally "cheeks") or *yarad* is paid either in actual camels or their equivalence in other categories of livestock, a woman's dia is not paid in actual camels. Blood money for other physical injuries, to both men and women, is not paid in actual she-camels, but the value is stated in she-camels.

In modern times, especially in cities, blood money is paid in cash *(mood)*, not in livestock *(nool)*. But the unit for measuring is still the value of a camel; therefore the expression cited above, *Geel waa geel wixii gooyaan waa geel* is valid for the present.

For Somali pastoralists, camels are still the basis of their wealth; a man's capital is equal to the number of camels he owns. The owner of one hundred camels is considered very rich.

Nin labaatan wiil liyo nimaan weli lamaani
lixdan nimay ufooftiyo niman layli raranaynin
marhadduu ninaba laasaneyn waxa u laacaaya
maxan kaga lulmoodaa adduun lumaya weeyaane
"He who fathered twenty sons, and one who is still alone,
He who owns sixty camels, and one who doesn't even have

a pack camel.
Since none of them will satisfy his ambition,
There is no point in worrying about a vanishing world.

This verse *(gabay)* expresses the pastoralist's attitude. Even in modern poetry or songs referring to the national independence of both Somalia and Djibouti, camels are used as a reference:

Magawdoo candhadii gollaha marisee
an maallo hasheenna maandeeq
Its udder is bursting with milk -
let us milk our she-camel, *maandeeq.*

The she-camels *maandeeq* (the one that satisfies the mind), that the poet is referring to is the national flag or national independence.

Many of the city people still own camels in the *miyi baadiye* for they believe that life in the cities is both uncertain and artificial. Anyone who lived in Djibouti during the blockade in the early forties remembers how many people suffered from the effects of starvation. Because of this, many people in the cities still keep one foot in the *miyi.*

The following poetic duel between Soodaan Idris and Cismaan Hande, one defending life in the city and the other defending life as camel owners, expresses the psychological conflict between the two modes of living.

Soodaan Idris:
Drajada adduun waa ninkii
dahab sameeyaaye
dadnna waxa lammaatiya
ninkii daara hoos galae
dibaddaa markaad gaadha buu
dacas ku fuulaaye
awr dabar la boodiyo intaad
adhi dabbaaleysid
ayuunbaad allaa daayinee
daayac noqotaaye
doqonniimo waa waxa tolkay
dooxxadaa dhigaye
magaalada hadduu degelahaa
dalaw ma gaadheen
waxaad i gula doodaysid waa
laguma daalaane

Sudan Idris:
To be the best in the world
is to accumulate gold,
the ultimate success of a man
is when he owns stone houses.
When you go out of the city,
all unpleasant things happen to you.
As long as you are keeping camels
and sheep,
by Allah the Eternal,
you will be at a loss.
It is because of their foolishness
that my clansmen are in the remote valleys.
If they could settle in the cities,
they could be in safety.
What you are arguing for is
not worth the effort.

Cismaan Hande:
Dirirtii talyaaniga markii
dayrka laga yaacay
ee daarihii laga tegiyo
dahabki hoos yeellay

Isman Hande:
During the Italian war when people
escaped from the walls of the town,
when stone houses and their contents
of gold were left behind,

adiguba dadkiibaad ahayd	you were one of those who
diiq ka soo baxaye	escaped in difficulty.
daaduun waxaa loolissaa	For destitute refugees
deero iyo cawle	the she-camels are milked.
duco nabiyadiibuu qabaa	It has been blessed by the prophets
dabac maxaw geeyey	He shouldn't have said anything against the she-camel, *dabac*.

The Camel's Effect on Somali Culture and Literature

One can confidently conclude that Somali culture is, for the most part, a camel culture and in particular that Somali literature is based on the camel rearing and breeding mode of life.

The Somali counting numbers are qualified with the word *hal*, she-camel. For example, "two things" in Somali is *laba hal;* the word *hal* will go with any number for qualification. In the same way the names of the days are based on milking times for livestock, of which camels are the most important. Two milking times, *laba caana maal*, make a day, *maalin*, since livestock for the most part are milked twice a day, early in the morning and early in the evening.

One could argue to an even greater extent that the Somali language itself has been shaped by the influence of the camel culture. A colleague of mine, who is planning to compile a new Somali dictionary, told me that he discovered, after listing the words in alphabetical order, that the words starting with the letter "G" are the most numerous. Then it came to my mind, since the word *geel* starts with the letter "G" and since alliteration played a great role in preserving all forms of Somali literature, many "G" words have been coined for that end. Though this is only a hypothesis there is surely a grain of truth in it. References are made to *geel* in every form of Somali literature, whether in proverbs, quotations, or different types of poetry. However, the influence of the camel culture is most evident in the basic Somali literature.

By basic literature I mean the literature based on camel or other livestock rearing such as i) the *shubaal*, watering song, ii) *jiib*, folkloric song, iii) *guux*, pastoralist "blues", iv) *maahmaahyo*, proverbs, and v) modern Somali poetry.

Shubaal, or the work song for watering animals
This genre of Somali literature contains six or seven vowels; because of its short meters, it is easily picked up and memorized by anyone, irrespective of age or sex. At the same time the *shubaal* genre forms the nucleus of

many longer Somali poetic genres, and since every pastoralist or herder memorizes a great deal of the *shubaal,* one could speculate that all Somali pastoralists are either poets or potential poets.

The *shubaal* genre is not only for amusement; it is one of the means by which Somali pastoralists educate their young in their way of life. When telling the young that order should be strictly watched and that each herd should be watered in its turn, the following verse is used:

Geelu geel fulay	The camels cannot overtake
gaadhi maaye	the camels that have already been watered
haka daba fulo	It should leave when it has its fill.

When the experienced herder is reminding the young and inexperienced herder of times past, he tells him in the following song that the world is an ever-changing process:

Ardaa guri yada	These ancient sites,
abuuriinada	and ruins
uun horaa degay	were occupied by ancients.
isna ka abaad	But they are no more
adnase ogow	and you should be aware of that.

Sometimes he expresses how, if you don't protect your camels with your firearms, you may lose to hostile clans:

In rag sara kacay	That men have stood up
siigada al kumay	dust has been blown up
seddexmaarra ha	and firearms
sinta laga lulay	are being taken up
siddaa ma ogtahay	are you aware of that.

The following verse is recited when expressing that there has never been peace when it comes to camel ownership:

Sidiiloo helay	Since camels came into possession
ragnna loo hiray	and men were repelled
loogu hadalyoo	there has been a quarrel over it
looguma heshiin	and there has never been a concord.

Sometimes a camel herder expresses his worries using the following verse:

Cirku mayeybuu	The sky, because of morning rain,
la ma dawyahay	it is dark.
anna murugiyo	And I, because of sadness,
maxay noqonbaan	and what the future holds,
la madoobahay	I am dark.

It is through the *shubaal* that a great part of the pastoralists' "educational system" is propagated; the rest is through other forms of work songs and other types of Somali traditional poetry of which the *jiib* is a very important one.

Jiib

The *jiib*, a genre which contains nine vowels, is used in most of the songs that are sung with the Somali folkloric dances such as *botor, seddexlay* and *riixa*. These folkloric dances and songs are only for the better times of the *gu* season. During the moonlit nights of that season, after the camel herders join the herders of other types of livestock, young people of both sexes stay out dancing and singing.

One of the best known folkloric songs that uses the *jiib* genre is the *riixa* (pushing one another). This name is because the dancers form two rows, one of young men, the other of young women, and move back and forth in a very elegant way during the dance. The camel herder checks whether the younger girls, whom he has not seen since the end of the last *gu* season, have grown up to be approached for marriage.

The camel herders, who make up the core of the dancers, expect each and every young girl in the village to come out for the dancing. They start singing with the following verse:

> *Inantaan soo janbalaq odhan*
> The girl that does not come readily for the dance
> *een sacabka kuu jebin*
> and does not clap her hands warmly,
> *wax la daba jajaba maaha*
> should not be sought after.

As in the *shubaal* genre, they express their views of tragedy and its effects on both humans and animals.

Marbuu geesi ooyaa	When a hero feels sorrow
waa marka geel la qaadaa	is when his camels get looted
gabankii jiray la gawraco	and their herders has been slaughtered.
marbay gaari ooydaa	When a good woman feels sorrow
wa markay geesi weydaa	is when she loses her brave husband
gocorbaas lagu gadaada	and is forced to remarry a very weak one.
marbu geelu ooyaa	When camels fell sorrow
waa marku maqasha waaya	is when they lose their baby camels
ee maqaarbaas lagu gadaadaa	and are deceived by hides erected on frames to look like real baby camels.

For them, camels are like intimate relatives or friends and they are affected by their happiness as well as their grief.

The season of the *gu* is the time when the camel herder looks for his future wife. It is only after marrying that he will be relieved of his responsibility as a camel herder. It is through the *jiib* that he expresses his appreciation for the girl of his choice. He tells her the length and breadth of the area he covered just to be near her.

Habsanay tima haldhaalay	O! the attractive one whose hair
hal kiyo hawdka jarareed	looks like the feathers of a male ostrich,
meella kaaga hadhimaaye	all the way from the Jarar area
halaha waan ku dabawadi	I won't stay far from you, I will drive my she-camels to wherever you go.

Jiib, like the first genre, *shubaal*, is widely used by the young camel herders to tell about their difficulties, exploits and expectations. But what is very interesting about this genre is that in many verses, and in different situations, camels are still the main reference; the singer even likens himself to the camel stallion:

Lo'ada baarqabkeedii	Cattle's stallion
waaka beerta lagu qodo	is used for ploughing the land;
geela baarqabkiisii	Camel's stallion
waata buulka lagu raray	is made a beast of burden.
adna baarqabkaagii	And your stallion
waakan beydda kuguwada	is the one who is dancing with you.

Many women's pastoralist songs are based on the *jiib* genre; however, the camel herders still dominate the scene in the quantity and the quality of the songs and the multiplicity of the dances. Both the *shubaal* and the *jiib* are group songs, but the *guux* genre is sung by individuals.

Guux

The *guux* contains about ten or eleven vowels, is exclusively composed, sung and propagated by the camel herders when they are still unmarried. Through this genre they express the frustration that results from their long isolation from their peer group and especially from the opposite sex, since girls never go with the *geelxer*.

The theme of the *guux* is mainly concerned with the camel herders' yearning for marriage. They complain about their exile with other herders in the remote corners of the camels' grazing lands.

Uustardheera ninlaa gudbada	A rifle is taken up by he who possesses it.
ameeta ninlaa huwada	A warm sheet of cloth is worn by he who has it.
aroos ninlaabaa hadh gala	And he who is wed rests well,
ee aroori anna ku hadhay	but I am left in the wilderness.

It is through the *guux* verses that the young herder appeals to his parents for permission to look for his future wife, or requests his father to arrange marriage for him.

Kuwii aabaha lahaa	Those whose fathers are still alive,
amma agoon xoole la ahaa	or those whose fathers died but left a multitude of
aroos yey wada galeen	livestock, were wed to beautiful girls,
ee aroori anna ku hadhay	but I am left in the wilderness.

I will call the *guux* a Somali pastoralist's "blues". The way he sings in his loneliness in the middle of the night, while blowing his traditional flute *(foodhin)* makes his colleagues feel sorry for his plight. But in some cases it is a way of keeping him awake to guard against nocturnal beasts of prey, like lions, that may venture over the thorn fence into the camels' midst.

Since the *geelxer* is an all male society, the verses they compose refer directly to sex or sexual organs - a topic that is taboo to talk about when the womenfolk are around. The following verse is explicitly referring to a physical lust which the herder blames on his personified male sexual organ:

Dhaban malahoo	It does not have cheeks
ka dhirbaaxi maayo	that I could slap.
feedha malahoo	It does not have ribs
ka fugsiinimaayo	that I could beat with my fists.
la i gal yoo	I am being disturbed
la i goondhabe	and am being hit hard
sida warrabe	as if a hyena
la ii qudqudhi	is constantly feeding upon my living body.

Sometimes he daydreams of his under-age beloved. He has been promised her hand in marriage, but on the condition that she grows to maturity so as to be in a position to tackle her responsibilities as a wife and mother.

Aabaheed bilanbuu yidhaa	Her father calls her *Bilan*
hooyadeed bilisay tidhaa	her mother calls her *Biliso*
anna baraar leegbaan idhaa	and I call her the one
laye baraar adhi wuu koraaye	who is as a baby sheep *(Baraar)*
ee baraarka haween ma koro	A baby sheep grows up,
	but a baby woman never grows up.

Because of his long association with camel herding, a herder may feel nostalgia for that way of life even after he marries.

Gaana dumarbaa laygu daray	I have been wedded to a very strong woman.
garaw la caanayn baaihelay	I have been fed with ungreased millet.
sidii geedkaan u dhadhay	I have been shrunk like a dead tree.
sidii gumartaan u uray	And I have smelled like a

ee geelasheenni maaragteen   *Gumar* (Acacia Oerfota) tree.
                                      Can you tell me where our herds are grazing?

As a genre *guux*, or *gunuunucas*, is confined to the extreme west of northern Somalia and the Republic of Djibouti where the names of famous composers - though most composers, like those of the *shubaal* and *jiib* genres, are anonymous - are remembered by the camel herders of the area. The composer of the verse above is Cawaale Bustaale, who remained unmarried for a long time.

Maahmaahyo (proverbs)
Together with the work songs, the folkloric songs and the *guux*, proverbs and other quotations refer to camels. Somali pastoralists stored their wisdom and stated their conclusions about the world around them through proverbs, many of which glorify the camel.

Geel nimanlahaynin waa magan.
He who does not own camels lives under the protection of others.
Geel nabad buu u abaarsadaa.
Camels' plight comes if there is no peace.
Naago ubadbay u abaarsadaa.
Women's plight comes if they don't have children.
Ragna aqoonlii buu u abaarsadaa.
And men's plight comes if they are ignorant.
Dhaari seddexba way kaxaysaa:
A false testimony takes three things away:
ragga xugunka,
It takes a men's fertile sperms away,
dumarkana xaylka,
it also takes women' fertile ova away,
geelana xoorka.
and it takes the camels' milking ability away.

For them, human fertility and propagation are only possible if enough milk can be secured. A camel herder can simply swear by the expression *"Wallaahidaan caana waayaa"*, - "By Allah, may I never have milk". To stay in a place where there are no camels is a waste of time:

Iga kici kobtaan geel ku dhalin   At a place where camels did not calve
kuudad xumadeeda   I will not stay.

For them, life is only worth living if one owns camels; a man who does not own camels when he dies will pass unnoticed.

Geel niman lahayn	For a man who doesn't own camels
geeridii warmaleh	the event of his death will pass unmarked.

Even in the next world, *aakhiro,* a man without camels will be at a disadvantage.

Aakhiro nimaan geel lahayn	In the next world a man who does not own camels
lama amaanayn	is despised.

There is no doubt that the Somalis' Islamic background contributed to their veneration of camels.

Ilal ibili lama soo dejeen	The Quranic verse
aayadii horae	wouldn't have been revealed
assaxaabi hii horabawey	but for the Prophet's Companion
kuintifaaceene	who made the best of use.

Modern Somali Poetry

How camel herding and camel ownership influenced the Somali way of life even after settling in urban centres is best illustrated in the modern Somali songs. They are based on the pastoralists' traditional poetic genres and camels are widely used as a reference.

Geel laba awr	For the she-camel to have two competing stallions
oo absiimada eesta	for mating
kuma sama	is not appropriate.
reerku laba oday	For a clan, two competing leaders
oo arrimiyaah	to lead
aadba kuma sama	is not appropriate.
loodu oon iyo	For cattle thirst
guul arooriyo	driving it for watering in a night
abaar kuma sama	and a draught are not appropriate.
anna aayaha	For my future
kaan ku eleleday	the one of whom I dreamt,
oon isweynaa	not to have him
waygu adagtahay	is unbearable.

The above verse has been put to music for a modern song; it is one of the most popular songs broadcast over Radio Djibouti. There are a multitude of other examples that could be used to illustrate how all the Somali poetic genres are being adapted for modern theatre and modern music.

The camels' grazing lands are still used as an artistic reference even in modern songs.

Sidii cirku hooray	Your beauty is reminiscent of grazing land on which
meel cossobloo	it rained recently
cadceed usoo	and on which a bright sun
baxdaatahay	shone.

To conclude, camel herding has dominated the Somali way of life. It has shaped the Somalis' destiny and greatly influenced their attitude towards themselves and towards others. It has left its greatest mark on their language and literature; definitely it will keep on influencing their life and actions. To understand the Somalis, one has to understand their culture; and to understand it one has to look back on their long association with camel herding and the mode of life that has sprung from it.

In fact, camels are not the most useful livestock. For immediate utility they cannot be compared with either sheep, goats or cattle. From these other types of livestock, people make butter, which they sell in the cities, and use the income to buy the things they need. But still, camels, like gold, are the standard unit for measuring everything that is of value in life.

NOTES

All the facts and verses in this paper are from the collections of Radio Djibouti Cultural Programmes, 1984-1987. The major contributors are:

1. Ahmed Aden Adadle, a poet and a great artist; age 72.
2. Omer Good Buuh, a poet, camel herder, folkloric dancer, *guux* composer and oralist; age 54.
3. Ismail Mahamoud Sugeh, an oralist; age 54.
4. Hassan Elmi, an oralist and author of major plays and theatrical pieces of very high quality. He contributed greatly to the emergence of the modern Somali song. More than anyone else, he used almost all the Somali pastoralist poetic genres in his modern songs. He composed the verse for the modern Somali song which I used to illustrate how the modern Somali song makes use of the traditional poetic genre; age 55.
5. Ibrahim Garabyare, one of the originators of the Somali modern song, a composer and singer who started his career as an artist in 1943 and is still active in both composing and singing; age 62.
6. I am very indebted to my colleague and friend, Omer Ma'llin, whose collection of poems and proverbs I used for illustrating the duel between the urbanized Somalis, represented by the late Sudan Idriss, and those who see camels as the best insurance, represented by the late Osman Hande.

DISCUSSANT'S REPORT

Frode Storås

In his paper, "Camel herding and its effects on Somali literature", Mohamed Abdillahi Rirash shows how the Somali pastoralists have a "camel complex". The importance of the camel in all aspects of life is shown through the extensive use of this animal in the literature, also as the basic unit of measuring value. Rirash, furthermore, shows the variety of camel husbandry in Somalia; the type of camel that is kept is that which is most appropriate for the particular environment.

Adaptation to environment is also a key point in the paper "Pastoralism at loggerheads" by Ayele Gebre Mariam. He shows how outside factors (such as wars) force the pastoralists to utilize alternative, non-pastoral resources. Thus, in spite of the cultural value of the camel ("camel complex"), the camel pastoralists are part of continuous by changing societies where the economic importance of the animals may vary. Still, cultural factors are decisive in how people define that is good life. If we want to raise the standard of living of the people (a common conclusion of all the papers in this workshop) we must have as a starting point the people's evaluation of what is a good life.

It is then not sufficient to focus only on the economic or veterinary side of livestock. The socio-cultural importance of livestock should not be underestimated. Pastoralists act in the context of a web of claims connecting individuals to a network of personal relations. These claims may involve giving and receiving of animals. Thus social value is one aspect of the value the pastoralists attribute to their livestock. The number may be more important than the quality of the animals.

All people have ideas about how life and society ought to be or should function, which emerge in interviews. (For instance the comparative value of camels and goats.) However, through observation we discover that reality is something different from ideas. As planners, we should try to understand the processes determining real life. We may then better understand how people adapt to changing contexts and situations and thereby reduce the risks of implementing development projects that end as failures; there are already too many of those. A regional perspective is required in order to prevent unintended implications from undermining the intended results.

The conflict of interest between governments and the pastoralists is well known in many areas. The lack of military and political control of nomads has been a determining factor behind many of the settlement programmes. Ayele, who stated that macro-political events had led to the impoverishment of pastoralists, said (in the discussion following this session), that if governments really want to help their people they will have to sacrifice privileges. If there is will, there is a way, he said.

Does "Development" Always Imply Progress? The Case of African Pastoralism[1]

Frode Storås

The life of nomadic pastoralists is often referred to either as "harsh" or "good". Those advocating development as a necessity implying drastic changes in the way of life of nomads (e.g. through settlement schemes), talk about nomadism as a harsh life in an eroding environment. On the other hand, the adaptation of nomadic pastoralists is also often characterized as being ecologically balanced and nomadic life as being free and good. A nomad from Africa would probably define e.g. wintertime in Furudal as very harsh and if he was in a position of planning the future for the people there, he may argue that it would be better for them to be moved to places of warmer climate. In other words: "we see the lives of others through lenses of our own grinding and...they look back on ours through ones of their own" (Geertz 1984:275).

Development projects involve many different and often conflicting interests. When development projects are discussed, however, the main rhetorical argument is always that the project is in the best interests of the people. Still, the ulterior motives can be meat production for urban areas, military control over roaming nomads, aid pushing in order to spend a quantity of money and so on. I am not arguing that such ulterior motives are always conflicting with what is in fact in the best interests of the people, but I feel that when development projects are discussed, one is generally unwilling to reveal all the interests that are involved. When plans are implemented, the factors or interests determining the decisions that are made are therefore hard to debate as long as they are not brought to the surface.

I once asked a group of nomads in East Africa what kind of development projects they were interested in. They answered that the best way I could help them was to tell the development organization and the government to stay away. I understood later that this answer was due to a feeling of losing control of their own future rather than a rejection of any projects. This is an experience which is well known among the many indigenous people around the world. The Sami people in Scandinavia, the

---

[1] These are the discussant's reflections upon the seminar.

Indians in America, the Aboriginals in Australia are among the so-called Fourth World people who have started to fight for defining and defending their own future.

Among the Fourth World people in Africa, as many of the nomadic pastoralists can be called, such movements have not yet come to the surface. Instead, they are destroyed for charitable purposes by development organizations (and, maybe, for other purposes by economical and political interests). The obvious distress many of these people are facing seems to be used to allow outsiders to interfere in whatever way they like with little respect for the dignity of the people. Furthermore, "harsh life", "ecological crises" and other expressions of aid rhetoric are used uncritically and are often exaggerated in order to underline the right to interfere.

These should be well-known arguments. But more than half a billion dollars have been spent on pastoral livestock schemes in Africa. A former Chief Economist at the International Livestock Centre for Africa in Addis Ababa, however, finds that development of water supplies, for example, or veterinary services, grazing schemes, creation of ranches, marketing schemes or livestock improvement programmes - all activities that have been pursued in pastoral projects - are managed so relatively well by the pastoralists that there has been little room for improvement (Jahnke 1982 cited in Aronson 1984). We therefore have to be realistic and admit the lack of success of our interventions.

Furthermore, the demand for land by non-pastoral people has continuously reduced valuable rangeland. One consequence of this has been an increasing number of people being sloughed off from the pastoral sector and the economic alternatives offered to them have in most cases proved not to be viable. In comparative studies of nomadic pastoralists and settled people in the northwestern corner of Kenya, we found that, however we measured their standard of living, the nomads were far better off (Broch-Due & Storås 1983, Broch-Due 1986).

Many reports have shown how well-intended development projects in drylands have resulted in an increasing number of people who have been settled in an unviable situation. Aid addiction has therefore become the ultimate consequence for too many people. As long as the economic alternatives to nomadic pastoralism are limited, we should be realistic and avoid projects that may lead to an aggravation of the nomadic pastoralists, situation.

Societies are complex, however, and people are not like machines whose reactions can be fully predicted. Projects aimed at solving one particular problem can be undermined by unintended results within or outside the problem area. New marketing possibilities (which, for instance, one had hoped would reduce land pressure), led to change from big stock to small stock rearing - which increased the threat to the environment. New wells providing water for communal use have undermined the traditional regulation of pastures made possible through individual or group control of the water points.

The different papers presented at this workshop have in a convincing way demonstrated the camel's adaptability to drylands. Camels are superior in economic terms and, furthermore, do not harm nature the way other domestic animals do. There are, however, some drawbacks with camel rearing. They have a low production rate and they need careful herding, since they easily stray and get lost and eventually become victims of prey. Even though they are resistant to drought and to the common epidemics affecting livestock, each animal is of such a value that one lost is a minor disaster.

Furthermore, in most pastoral societies security - the social, juridical and economic respects - is based on a wide network of personal relations.

These relations are constructed on principles derived from kinship and affinity and other institutional frameworks. The translation of these principles into effective social relations is a continuous process in which livestock become very crucial as gifts, or as food offered to uphold (or be invested in) social relations. Unless these relationships are maintained, they will crumble away (Storås, 1987).

In pastoral societies where security is based on such a system, big animals are used for the most important relationships only, while the fast to reproduce and relatively less valuable small animals enable people to maintain a wide network of personal relations. To handle these relations with the use of camels would be like running one's economy with one-thousand dollar notes.

Factors such as these may explain why some pastoralists are reluctant to change from small stock and cattle to camel rearing, in spite of the obvious superiority of camels. But no societies are static. All through history they have been exposed to changing situations which they have chosen or been forced to adjust; and not all societies have felt this as progress (cf Mariam in this volume). Recent changes implemented by development organizations have also not always been felt as progress.

In aid rhetoric, the word "development" is used as a synonym for "progress". This confusion of development and progress seems often to hold off a thorough debate on the possible negative implications of projects. Even in cases where the results of basic research are available, such a debate is often avoided. Basic research on how societies function on a different scale, however, can never guarantee success of a project, but may reduce the risks of failures. The condition, of course, is that the reports are studied and the results debated and taken into account.

Development planners seem often not be willing, or able, to learn from reports and from failures. Or maybe it is not a question of learning, but rather a question of not revealing the different interests behind the projects? Unless these often conflicting interests are brought to the surface, a sustainable development where the people are in the centre (Hjort, this volume) will be hard to achieve.

REFERENCES

Aronson, D.R. 1984: "Pastoralism in Contemporary Development Perspective", in: *Nomadic Peoples*, No 16.

Broch-Due, V. and Storås, F. 1983: "The Fields of the Foe. Factors Constraining Agricultural Output and Farmers Capacity for Participation. A Socio-Anthropological Case Study of Household Economy among the Inhabitants on Katilu Irrigation Scheme, Turkana, Kenya", *NORAD Report.*

Broch-Due, V. 1986: "From Herds to Fish. And from Fish to Food Aid", *NORAD Report.*

Geertz, C. 1984: "Anti anti-relativism", in: *American Anthropologist, 86.*

Hjort af Ornäs, A. 1988: "Sustainable Subsistence in Arid Lands; The Case of Camel Rearing." (This volume).

Mariam, A.G. 1988: "Pastoralism at loggerheads." (This volume).

Storås, F. 1987: "Intention or Implication - the effects of Turkana social organization on ecological balances." Paper presented at the workshop on *Changing Rights in Property and Problems of Pastoral Development.* Manchester.

Traits and Calf Behaviour in Bikaneri Breed of Camels

N.D. Khanna

Out of a world camel population 17.44 million, India possesses 1.10 million (FAO Yearbook, 1985), almost all of which are found in the North Western region of the country. Rajasthan State alone accounts for 72%. The increase in numbers (Table 1) has almost doubled between 1951 and 1985.

Indian camels, both baggage and riding camels, are of the dromedary type *(Camelus dromedarius)*. Some distinct breeds, classified according to body characteristics, include Bikaneri, Jaisalmeri, Sindhi, Marwari, Mewati and Kutchi. A small number of double-humped camels *(Camelus bactrianus)* are also found in the Ladhak region (cold desert) of the country.

BIKANERI BREED - CHARACTERISTICS

The home ground of this breed is the Bikaner district of Western Rajasthan, which is part of the Thar desert. The animals, known for their draft power, endurance and docility, are heavily built, the adult weight varying from 450 kg to 680 kg (Table 2). The physical characteristics of the Bikaneri breed are described in Table 3. The height of adult animals at the withers is 2-2.2 metres. The colour varies from light sandy to dark blackish brown and the reddish brown ones are the most highly prized.

Bikaneri camels generally have a short, hairy coat, although the "Jipra" strain have comparatively more abundant tufts of hair around eyes, ear, neck and under jaws, as well as thick eyelashes. The body is elongated and massive, the head slightly dome shaped. The forehead is well marked with a depression above the eyes and there is a prominent crest. The nose ridge tilts upwards. Ears are small, hairy and erect. The neck, medium to long and curved, gives the head graceful carriage. The hump is very well developed both in males and females, dome shaped and situated centrally on the back. Both fore and hind legs are long, strong and well muscled; the rib cage broad and well arched; hind quarters drooping; tail short with small tufts of hair switch at the end; testicles well developed and high-up on the groin. The udder of lactating females is well developed and is finely suspended at the hind part of the abdomen, with the milk vein being very prominent.

Most of the following observations on production, reproduction, physical, physiological and biochemical characteristics of the Bikaneri breed were made at the National Research Centre on Camel, Bikaner, which was established in July, 1984 by the Indian Council of Agricultural Research, New Delhi.

PRODUCTION TRAITS

Body weights and growth rate
The body weights of Bikaneri animals, according to age group, (presented in Table 2) show the maximum weight gains ranging from 527 to 686 kg. Calves 0-6 months old gained 610 g per day, while those aged 2-3 years gained 236 g (Table 3).

Physical measurements (leg length, girth circumference, height at withers, neck length) were measured in 62 growing animals of two age groups (Table 4). The preliminary observations indicated that the pattern of growth in both sexes was comparable up to puberty.

Birth weight
The average birth weight of female calves was 39.77 ± 5.32 kg, that of male calves 41.95 ± 7.7 kg while the overall mean was 41.02 ± 0.20 kg. The calves born to dams in the first parity were lightest (38.84 ± 5.19 kg) while heaviest calves were born to dams in the fifth parity (Table 5).

Age at first service
The average age at first service proved to be 1,390 ± 25.0 days, though it was much higher in the early years of the farm of the National Research Centre on Camel.

Age at first calving
The average age at first calving was found to be 1,882 ± 28.67 days.

Gestation period
Parity and sex of calf had no significant effect on the gestation period. There was, however, significant effect of season. The overall mean gestation period was 389.3 ± 0.08 days.

Inter-calving period
The inter calving period ranged from 700 to 800 days.

Genetic studies
The heritability estimates for birth weight was 0.5666 ± 0.19, age at first service 0.3114 ± 0.56, age at first calving 0.1984 ± 0.07 and gestation length 0.7035 ± 0.21 (Table 6). The correlations between birth weight and gestation period revealed an environmental correlation of 0.4589 while value for

phenotypic and genotypic correlations were 0.0136 ± 0.0523 and -0.2389 ± 0.2125 respectively.

Physiological and Biochemical parameters

Pulse rate and respiration rate of animals of different age groups were recorded twice a month throughout the year. The pulse rate ranged from 36 to 82 per minute in different seasons and was relatively lower in animals above 3 years of age. The respiratory frequency ranged from 7-20 per minute.

Haematological studies were conducted on 96 animals (Table 7). The variability due to sex was not significant. Eight biochemical constituents of blood viz., alkaline phosphatase, acid phosphatase, lactate dehydrogenase, glutamic oxalacetic transaminase (SGOT), glutamic pyruvic transaminase (SGPT), bilirubin, sodium and potassium were analyzed (Table 8).

BREEDING

The calving rate during 1986 was 60%. Three services per conception were required. The sex ratio for male and female calves was 39:61 (1986). This was significantly different from 1985 data which gave a ratio of 62.5:37.5. The sex ratio of calves during the last 11 years was 54:46. There was significant variation in the sex ratio of the newly born calves from year to year. Data on 904 births recorded during 1961-85 revealed that maximum births were recorded in the months of January and February followed by March, December, April, May, November and October. No birth was recorded in the months of June, July, August and September (Table 9). Two cases of congenital defects were recorded in 1985.

The breeding season in camel starts in India from mid-October to March. The males exhibit optimum rut during December to February. An analysis was made to study variability in copulation time. The results revealed that it varied from sire to sire and month to month.

A study was made to find out period of descent of testes and development of scrotal sacs in the male Bikaneri camel calves. It was observed that scrotal pouch and testes were not present at birth. However, a dark-coloured area demared with medium *raphae* was present a little below the anus where the scrotal sac developed in due course of time. The scrotal sac took from 66 to 106 days to develop (the average was 86.8 ± 15.7 days). There was no uniform pattern for the descent of the testicles. In some animals both testicles descended together while in others either the left or the right testicle descended first (Table 10). There was evidence that during the warmer months the descent was accelerated.

HORMONAL STUDIES

Sera were analysed for testosterone, progesterone, estradiol, thyroxine (T_4) and triiodothyronine (T_3) using R.I.A.. The results indicated that the breeding season had a marked influence on the hormonal level. The steriod hormones were significantly higher during the rutting season whereas thyriod hormones were higher during the non-rutting season, but T_4:T_3 was almost double during the rutting season. The hormonal studies on pregnant female revealed that females bearing male calves had relatively lower estradiol concentration (76.5 ± 10.8 pg/ml) than those carrying a female foetus (112.3 ± 19.6 pg/ml). On the other hand, progesterone level was slightly higher in dams carrying a male foetus (5.13 ± 0.69 ng/ml) than in those carrying a female foetus (4.45 ± 0.28 ng/ml).

An experiment was made on nine heifers, aged 2-3 years, concerning the effect of FSH on lowering the age at first calving. It was revealed that, after injection of FSH, all heifers exhibited oestrus and were successfully mated. However, full-term pregnancy was carried in only five animals.

MORTALITY

Mortality data from 1975 to 1986 were tabulated (Table 11). The mortality risk was highest for the 0-3 months age group and conspicuously higher during peak summer months. The mortality data further revealed that 17.40% deaths were due to disorders of the digestive system, 19.25% due to respiratory problems, 1.80% to disorders of the urinary system 22.00% were surgical cases, 6.10% died due to accidents and 23.50% from unspecified causes.

CAMEL HAIR

The fineness of camel hair ranged between 26.0 to 38.0 μ. The coefficient of variation of the fibre fineness ranged from 55 to 60%, indicating high variability. The proportion of medullated fibres was 53 to 78%. The length of the fibres ranged from 51 to 67 mm. The initial ph was 7.02. The tenacity range was 14.75 to 19.35 g/tex. The wet strength of camel hair was lower than that of wool. The camel hair blended slivers exhibited highest sliver strength of 19.0 and 13.09. The strength of camel hair yarn was 1.63 to 2.24 g/tex., while that strength of camel hair-wool (60/40 and 40/60 blends) were 3.08 and 2.68 g/tex respectively. The maximum elongation at break was noted in 60/40 camel hair-wool blends which was 18.6%, while that for other blends was in the region of 12 to 16% (Table 12).

BEHAVIOUR PATTERN OF CAMEL CALVES FROM BIRTH TO ONE MONTH OF AGE

At birth the calf in normal parturition assumed a sternal position with head slightly dropping towards the ground. The dam nosed and sniffed the calf but did not lick it. The new-born calf made repeated attempts to raise itself until finally, the hind legs flexed sufficiently for it to stand. It took about 30-50 minutes on average for the calf to stand (the range being 20 to 90 minutes). The heart rate at birth was 130-140/minute, which dropped to 100-120/minute after an hour. The rectal temperature, which at birth was 36-38 °C (37-38 °C after one hour) stabilized between 36.5 to 38 °C at about 1 month of age, depending upon the ambient temperature. Similarly, the respiration rate (at birth 30-42/minute, 28-36/minute after one hour) stabilized to 18-12/minute at one month of age. The pulse, at birth 116-128/minute, stabilized at 65-75/minute after 1 hour.

Initially, the calf's movement was unsteady with staggering gait. The young animal kept its forelegs sloping forward with its hind legs stretched behind so as to maintain balance. The movements became normal after 10-12 hours and the calf started following its mother. The first urination was 60-80 minutes and the first defecation 10-45 minutes after birth.

In general, the multiparous females showed an immediate maternal instinct unlike the first calvers. The calf generally began to suckle 60-90 minutes after birth. The time interval later became 1-3 hours and, as the calf advanced in age 3-6 hours. In the initial stages the calf had a tendency to suckle the same teat on the same side again and again; however, as it gathered strength, it used all four teats.

One hour after birth, the camel calf showed an ability to raise itself, as well as investigating its environment.

Camel calves were observed to be polyphasic in their rest, play and sleep; brief naps, then play or a period of activity followed by sleep were common behaviour. The posture of sleep was lateral recumbency. As the calf grew, it would relax at times by squatting on its chest pad by its mother's side.

TABLES

Table 1. *Trend in Camel Population in India (in thousand)*

Year	Population
1951	629
1956	776
1961	703
1966	1,028
1972	1,109
1977	1,063
1982	1,050
1985	1,100

Table 2. *Maximum Body Weights (kg) of Bikaneri Camels at Different Age Intervals*

Birth weight	41.0	5-6 years	546.2
6-12 months	243.0	6-7 years	606.0
1-2 years	317.0	7-8 years	607.8
2-3 years	376.0	8-9 years	647.2
3-4 years	517.4	9-10 years	686.5
4-5 years	527.1	10 years & above	686.6

Table 3. *Body Weight Gain Per Day (g)*

Age group	Average daily gain
0-6 months	610
6-12 months	381
1-2 years	244
2-3 years	236

Table 4. *Physical Measurements (cm) of 62 Bikaneri Camels*

	1 year	4 years
Leg length	114,7 ± 8,3	145,0 ± 4,4
Girth diameter	151,7 ± 5,5	206,0 ± 6,4
Height at withers	157,7 ± 2,5	202,3 ± 1,5
Neck length	84,7 ± 1,5	114,6 ± 3,7

Table 5. *Parity-wise Average Birth Weight of Camels*

	Average birth weight (kg)
First calver	38.84 ± 5.19
Second calver	41.61 ± 5.47
Third calver	41.70 ± 6.06
Fourth calver	42.35 ± 5.19
Fifth calver	44.39 ± 5.47

Table 6. *Heritability Estimates of Some Traits of Camels at the Farm of the National Research Centre of Camels, Bikaner*

Traits	Heritability
Birth weight	0.5666 ± 0.19
Age at first service	0.3114 ± 0.56
Age at first calving	0.1984 ± 0.07
Gestation length	0.7035 ± 0.21

Table 7. *Some Haematological Values of 96 Camels at the Farm of the National Research Centre of Camels, Bikaner*

Haemoglobin	13.29 ± 0.84 g%
RBC	$12.10 \pm 1.43 \times 10^{12}/l$
WBC	$8.29 \pm 1.33 \times 10^{9}/l$
PCV	36.91 ± 4.96%
MCV	$29.51 \pm 4.07\ \mu m^3$
MCH	11.08 ± 1.24 pg
MCHC	36.52 ± 4.52%
Platelets	$228.63 \pm 90.44 \times 10^{9}/l$

Table 8. *Some Biochemical Constituents of Blood in 96 Camels at the Farm of the Nation Research Centre on Camel, Bikaner*

Alkaline phosphatase	22-199 IU/l
Acid phosphatase	8.3-48 IU/l
Lactate dehydrogenase	44-116 IU/l
SGOT	1.5-53 IU/l
SGPT	3.5-26 IU/l
Bilirubin	0.36-3.0 mg/dl
Sodium	125-175 meq/l
Potassium	5.0-8.6 meq/l

Table 9. *Numbers of Calves Born at Different Months at the National Research Centre on Camel During 1961-1985*

Month	Male Calves	Female Calves	Sex ratio total
January	159	135	294
February	154	122	276
March	78	61	139
April	24	23	47
May	7	4	11
October	1	2	3
November	4	3	7
December	57	70	127
Total	484	420	904

Table 10. *Development of Scrotal Sac and Descent of Testes (days)*

Scrotal sac	86.8 ± 16.0
Right testicle	193.1 ± 54.7
Left testicle	195.2 ± 37.4
Both testicles (together)	170.7 ± 23.0
Both testicles (left first)	271.3 ± 29.2
Both testicles (right first)	225.0 ± 44.5

Table 11. *Pooled Mortality in Bikaneri Camels*

Age group	Camel days		Mortality (per 1,000 camel days)	
	1975-85	1986	1975-85	1986
0-3 months	21,867	2,524	1.42	0.79
3-36 months	233,320	26,870	0.18	0.03
Above 36 months	370,353	42,906	1.09	0
Pooled	625,540	72,300	0.17	0.04

Table 12. *Fibre Characteristics of Camel Hair in Bikaner*

Fibre length	51-67 mm
Fibre diameter	26-38 μ
Medulation	53-78%
Tenacity	15-19 g/tex
Sliver Strength	1,63-2,24 g/tex
Elongation at Break	12-16%
(Camel hair & blends)	

South American Camelids Raising and Reproduction in the High Andes

Julio Sumar

Introduction

When people talk about camels, they have in mind the Bactrian and the dromedary camels of Asia and Africa, for many it is a surprise to learn that there are indigenous camels in South America. In fact, there are two endemic domestic camelids, the alpaca *(Lama pacos)* and the llama *(Lama glama)*, and two wild species, the vicuña *(Lama vicugna)* and the guanaco *(Lama guanicoe)*.

Camels of the Old and New World belong to the family *Camelidae* in the ruminant sub-order *Artiodactyla*. They are usually separated from the other ruminants as *Tylopoda* (pad-footed): instead of hooves they have callous pads ending in claws. In the Old World there are two types of camels, known today as *Camelus dromedarius* (dromedary) and *Camelus bactrianus* (Bactrian camel).

The fossil records indicate that the *Camelidae* family originated and developed in Western North America about 16 million years ago, spread via land bridges into Asia and South America and finally became extinct in their original homeland (Koford, 1957). All the members of the *Camelidae* family live in very harsh environments: the one-humped camel is well adapted to hot arid desert regions from India in the east to Mauretania and Mali in the west: the two-humped camel is found today in the cold deserts and semi-arid areas from the Caspian Sea across central Asia to Manchuria.

The South American camelids occupy mostly high altitude areas in the Andean mountains of South America, although not exclusively so. Karyotypes of the Old and New World forms have shown a notable similarity, even though they have developed numerous different phenotipic characteristics. Taylor *et al* (1968) found no differences in the karyotype of the guanaco, the Bactrian camel and the dromedary. They found a modal chromosome number of 74 for the three species, a similar number to that found in the llama, alpaca and vicuña by Benirschke (1967). More recently, Bunch and Foote (1983) found not only a similarity between the karyotypes of the llama and the Bactrian camel but also that the banding pattern of the individual chromosomes were similar.

In addition, members of the Old and New World camelids have common both anatomical and physiological characteristics. The anatomy of the fore-stomach in these animals is distinctly different from that of Ruminantia. Motility characteristics are dissimilar and the timing of rumination and eructation in the course of the motility cycle differs from those of the reticulo-rumen of ruminants. They have numerous endocrine cells in the stomach wall, which may play an important role during adaptation to extreme environmental conditions. Utilization of endogenous urea-N and of water is exceptional (von Engelhardt *et al* 1984). In regard to reproductive physiology, all members of the species are "induced or reflex ovulators" and almost all the embryos implant in the left uterine horns. (Later, we will discuss other reproductive mechanisms in these superb animals.)

Since the most important species of the South American camelids, from the socio-economic point of view, are the alpaca and llama (the domestic species), I will deal with these species in more detail.

HABITAT OF THE SOUTH AMERICAN DOMESTIC CAMELIDS

Along the western border of South America runs a high mountain chain called the Andes (or Cordillera de los Andes). In the central Andes, camelids have long been associated with the *puna*, a high altitude grassland 3,700 to 4,800 metres above sea level, with low atmospheric pressure. The air is consequently less dense, and less able to absorb and retain radiant energy. There are drastic differences in day-time and night-time temperatures (Koford, 1957). The average annual temperature at 4,000 metres is about 7 °C ± 17, which means that there is frost 300 nights a year. Every 100 metres above the 4,000 metres level, the temperature drops 0.5 °C to 1 °C, resulting in frost practically every night of the year above 4,700 metres.

The average rainfall in this region is between 500-900 mm from December through April; however, the rainy season and the amount of rainfall vary in each area every year, and prolonged drought is not uncommon. These conditions make farming a high risk activity, fundamentally limited to crops domesticated by the ancient Peruvians that depend on specific ecological conditions found in very limited areas. Animal raising based on grazing the natural pasture is less risky as well as a more stable source of food, than cultivating crops.

The main phyto-ecological formation of the *puna* is a sort of savanna, characterized by grasses growing in tufts (*Festuca, Stipa, Calamagrostis*). Particularly in the moist areas richer in humus, there is a lawn-like growth of *Poa, Muhlembergia* and *Distichia* grasses (Tosi, 1960).

SOCIAL AND ECONOMIC IMPORTANCE

There are an estimated 25 million hectares of *puna* in the Andean highlands of Peru, western Bolivia, northwest Argentina and northern Chile. The alpaca and llama are specially important because, even though they are also found lower, their adaptability to high altitudes makes it possible to rear them above 4,000 metres, where crops cannot be grown and sheep and cattle cannot be profitably raised.

Some 300,000 peasant families make their livelihood from raising these species. Camelid fibre (this is the correct name to distinguish it from sheep wool) is very valuable to the textile industry; llama and alpaca meat is the only source of animal protein available to the inhabitants of the high Andes; and the pelts are used for furriery. Also, the llama is the only South American camelid used as a pack animal.

Alpacas are mainly bred for fibre production and at present Peru produces an average of 3,400 tonnes of alpaca fibre annually, (more than 80% of the world total. Meat production for immediate consumption, or storage as sun dried "charqui" (jerked beef) is considerable and could be increased.

The llama produces a coarser and stronger fibre than the alpaca that is used mainly for carpets and coarser textiles. Llamas, which are not sheared as regularly as alpacas, are kept as pack animals. They can transport loads weighing 25-30 kg (55-66 pounds) over distances of 15-20 km daily (Flores-Ochoa, 1977).

The peasant families of the Peruvian highlands own 80% of the total domestic population of camelids; the rest are found in different types of associations and cooperatives and on small, privately-owned properties.

Table 1 shows the estimated numbers and types of South American camelids.

Despite their usefulness to humans, the breeding and management of these native species has been very poor and very little attention has been paid to their improvement. However, their productivity is limited by a number of factors. Among these are a harsh natural environment; a deteriorating feed supply caused by overgrazing; low animal productivity, due to lack of knowledge about their reproductive physiology; the absence of breeding programmes and the presence of infectious and parasitic diseases.

Llamas and alpacas have survived because they are an essential element of the Andean culture (Orlove, 1980). Breeding and herd management procedures, which are determined by a mosaic of traditional and hispanic techniques, may appear backward or irrational to outsiders. The system of livestock production might seem inefficient and unproductive, and it is hard to explain why the local herders resist technological improvements. However, the highland Peruvian herders are responsive to change, if it is properly conceived and directed.

REPRODUCTIVE PHYSIOLOGY

Since most reproductive physiology studies have been done with the alpaca *(Lama pacos)* and only few with the llama, I will refer mostly to reproduction of the alpaca and only where necessary to the llama.

Male reproduction

Puberty
At birth, the penis is completely adherent to the prepuce. The adherences disappear gradually along with the growth of the animal under the influence of testosterone. At 1 year of age, the males show sexual interest in the females; however, only about 8% of the males show a complete liberation of the penis-prepuce adherences and are capable of copulation (Sumar *et al* 1983). At 2 years of age, approximately 70% of the males have a liberation of the adherences, and 100% at 3 years. Precocious behaviour and early mating are considered to be desirable traits in genetic selection programmes. Future sires are those that do not have prepuce-penis adherences as yearlings. However, the general practice is to use the males for reproduction at 3 years of age.

Sexual behaviour
Field observations have shown a *sui generis* behaviour of the alpacas. The male begins courting by running behind the female whether or not she is on heat. If the female is in hear, she will let the male mount her and she will adopt a seated position. Copulation will last for 5-50 minutes. During copulation the male makes a guttural sound, in contrast to the female, who remains submissive. Sometimes females will seat themselves next to a mating couple as a sign of also being on heat. At the beginning of the breeding season, when the males first join the females, the males show intense sexual activity, copulating up to 18 times per day. Recent studies indicate that the deposition of semen during normal copulation, is inside the uterus (Sumar, 1983).

Semen production
The collection of semen is complicated by the position of the mating animals. Mogrovejo (1952) reported the collection of semen from 50 males, using artificial vaginal sleeves which were recovered after copulation. San

Martin *et al* (1968) utilized vaginal pessaries or sponges to collect semen from 190 males, reporting that 20% of the males did not have spermatozoa. However, both forms of semen collection are questionable, since they interfere with normal copulation and contaminate the semen. Also, in both studies the volume of semen ejaculated was highly variable, fluctuating between 0.4 and 6.6 ml.

The use of the electro-ejaculator was reported by Fernández-Baca and Calderón (1966) and seems to be the most adequate means of semen collection. Nevertheless, during the electrical stimulus, the semen is contaminated with urine and its quality is variable, with a sperm concentration fluctuating between 1,000 and 255,000/mm^3. Recently, Sumar and Leyva (1981) reported the use of the artificial vagina inside an alpaca dummy, obtaining up to 12.5 ml of high quality semen, with high motility and more than 600,000 sperms/mm^3. The semen of the alpaca is highly viscous, making difficult the separation of spermatozoa from seminal plasma and the estimation of sperm concentration by conventional methods. Different enzymes are being tested which liquefy the plasma without damaging the sperm. Due to the high viscosity of the seminal plasma, sperm motility is slow compared to that of other domestic species. Many previously reported studies have not taken this into account in reporting the low motility of alpaca and llama semen.

Experimental evidence with the use of the urethral fistula (Kubicek, 1974) and the artificial vagina indicates that ejaculation is a continuous process, with a uniform semen quality from the beginning to the end of the copulation.

Female reproduction

Puberty
The majority of females show sexual receptivity at 12 months of age. Ovarian activity begins at 10 months, with the presence of follicles of 5 mm or more. The nutritional level influences the beginning of puberty. Young female alpacas of 12-13 months showed oestrus similar to adult alpacas.

In a study to evaluate the effects of body weight during the breeding season on the reproductive performance in 280 female yearling alpacas, it was determined that a highly significant (P<0.001) relationship exists between body weight at breeding and parturition rates (Leyva and Sumar, 1981). For each kilogram gained, there was a 5% increase in parturition; but when body weight exceeded 33 kg, the percentage of open females was relatively independent of the body weight. Under present management and breeding systems, only 50% of yearling alpaca reach 33 kg of liveweight at breeding time; with a better nutritional level, 80% could do so. In the tropics, puberty has been affected by environmental conditions, but a relationship with body weight still exists. In Peru female alpacas are bred at 2 years of age, reflecting inadequate nutrition and management.

Breeding season
Studies with alpacas and llamas in their natural habitat in the highlands of southern Peru showed that the breeding season lasts from December to March. These are the warmest months, with sufficient rain and abundant green forage. However, in those farms where males and females are together all year, as occurs with the herds in peasant communities, lambing occurs from December to March. This also happens with the wild species such as the vicugna and guanaco that are considered seasonal in terms of reproductive activity (Franklin, 1978). When the females are kept separate from the males and copulation is allowed only once a month, both males and females are sexually active during the entire year. Ovulation and fertilization rates, along with embryo survival, were not affected significantly by the season of the year (Fernández-Baca *et al* 1971).

Experimental observations show that the continuous association of females and males inhibited sexual activity of the males and even caused it to disappear altogether (Fernández-Baca *et al* 1972). Factors responsible for the onset and cessation of sexual activity under natural conditions are unknown. Environmental factors, in addition to visual and olfactory stimulation, could be of influence via the central nervous system. It is well documented that the effect of external stimulation on sexual behaviour is more pronounced in the male than in the female. For instance, changing the teaser cow is an effective way to increase sexual activity in a sluggish male (Coolidge effect). Novoa *et al* (1970) developed a breeding system for alpacas, changing the breeding males each week for another group of males, enhancing the mating rate in the herd and, consequently increasing the lambing percentage.

Oestrus and Ovulation
Female alpaca do not have oestrus cycles like other domestic species. When not exposed to a male, they can have a continuous oestrus, up to 36 days, with short periods of male rejection that could last 48 hours (San Martin *et al* 1968). The signs of heat in alpacas and llamas are not well defined and are subject to a high degree of individual variation.

The female alpaca or llama in heat adopts a special pattern of behaviour in the presence of the males. They may take the prone position when the male is approaching them, or they may approach a male that is copulating with another female and adopt the prone position. In other cases, the male follows the female for a short time, then mounts her and finally the female takes the prone position. It is also common to see some females in heat mounting other females.

The alpaca and llama, like the rabbit, cat, ferret, and other members of the *Mustelidae,* show induced or reflex ovulation. The same mechanism have been found in the Old World camels. In the alpaca ovulation occurs 26 hours after copulation and 24 hours after when hCG (500-700 i u, i m) is used. One milligram of luteinizing hormone was effective in inducing ovulation; a dose 4-8 micrograms of GnRH was also necessary to provide the adequate stimulus for ovulation (Sumar and Bravo. 1981). Spontaneous ovulation occurs in 10 - 42% of the females, especially during the height of the breeding season. This is probably caused by the "presence of the male" on isolated females, similarly to the "ram effect". Recently the team of researchers of "La Raya" Research Station in Peru reported that alpaca and bull semen induced ovulation in alpacas in heat without mating, proposing the presence of an "ovulation induction factor" (OIF) of unknown biochemical composition. The same mechanism has been found in the Bactrian camel of China (Chen *et al* 1985).

Under existing management conditions in Peru, failure to ovulate could be an important factor contributing to a low reproductive rate. Sumar and Bravo (1982a) found that 38% of the adult female alpacas ovulated late (30-72 hours after copulation) and that 8.1% failed to ovulate. In the case of alpaca yearlings, 36% ovulated late and up to 35% failed to ovulate.

Multiple ovulation occurred in 10% of the cases after natural mating and in 20% of the cases with the application of gonadotrophins, but twins born alive are extremely rare. Implantation of twins occasionally occurs and may last during the first 40 days of pregnancy, but only one case has been reported to last during the first 10 months of pregnancy in Peru (Sumar, 1980). There are no marked differences in the ovulation rate between ovaries, although the right ovary ovulated 50.9%, the left 47.4% and 1.7% of the animals ovulated from both ovaries (Fernández-Baca *et al* 1973).

Corpus luteum formation and function
Previously, it was believed that the sterile matings were always followed by a long period of pseudo-pregnancy. This is not the case. After mating with a vasectomized male in alpacas and llamas, a functional corpus luteum was formed. Progesterone was secreted from day 5 and reached maximum concentration of 10-20 nmol/l on day 7-8. A rapid decline in progesterone levels occurred on day 9-10 in connection with repeated surge releases of prostaglandins F2. Oestradiol levels were >100-200 pmol/l during oestrus when the animals were mated. A temporary increase was detected in connection with the rise in progesterone levels in the early luteal phase. With this exception, of oestradiol stayed low, 20-40 pmol/l during the luteal phase, but rose in most animals after luteolysis to 40-60 nmol/l (Sumar *et al*, in press).

Sumar and Leyva (1981a) studied the role of the corpus luteum during pregnancy in alpacas. The study included the surgical removal of the ovary that presented the corpus luteum or simply the ablation of only the corpus luteum, with the control being a sham operated alpaca with the ovary and corpus luteum intact. In the first two treatments, from the first month of pregnancy up to ten months, cases of abortion occurred: with ovarian removal or enucleation of corpus luteum at 11 months of pregnancy the calves were born alive, but with low birth weight, and most died. This means that in the alpaca the corpus luteum is the major source of progesterone throughout the pregnancy period. Similar results have been found with the llama (Sumar and Bravo, 1982).

Fertility rates and embryonic mortality
In a study conducted by Fernández-Baca *et al* (1970), more than 80% of the ova recovered 3 days after mating were in the process of dividing; and only 50% of the fertilized ova survived for more than 30 days of gestation. During the first months, embryo mortality is higher in alpacas than in other domestic species, and seems to be a serious reproductive problem of this species. No factors have been identified as causing this high rate.

Diagnosis of pregnancy
It is important to mention that in practice, pregnancy diagnosis is done by external palpation at 8 months of pregnancy, a process at which most herdsmen are highly skilled; but for a good reproductive management of the herds is very late. Recently, the accuracy of three methods of pregnancy diagnosis were compared: ultrasound, rectal palpation supplemented with ballottement and oestrus behaviour using teaser males. The same animals were used for all three methods.

Using teaser males in alpacas, 84 and 88% accurate diagnosis was obtained at 70 and 125 days of pregnancy, respectively. In llamas, 85 and 95% accuracy was obtained at 75 and 125 days of pregnancy, respectively. Using the ultrasound method, the accuracy of pregnancy diagnosis was 92 and 100% at 80 and 75 days of gestation in alpacas and llamas respectively. This accuracy fell to 60% as the stage of pregnancy increased in both species. By rectal palpation, supplemented with ballottement (ballottement in younger animals, due to the small size of the pelvic opening), 100% accuracy was obtained.

In alpacas, rectal palpation was statistically more accurate ($P<0.05$) than ultrasound and oestrus behaviour; these two methods failed to differ statistically. In llamas, no differences were found among animal species in any of the methods tested. The ultrasound method is as accurate in camelids as it is in sheep. This method can be recommended as a management tool, to diagnose pregnancy as early as 75 days post-mating (Alarcón *et al*, in press).

Gestation and parturition
San Martin *et al* (1968) found a long gestation period of 342-346 for alpacas. Almost all fetuses are found to be implanted in the left uterine horn, even though both ovaries ovulate to an equal degree, indicating that the embryo originating in the right side emigrates to the left horn in order to survive (Fernández-Baca *et al* 1973). The reason for this unique internal migration and low rate of embryo implantation in the right horn of the uterus remain a mystery. One study of the differential luteolytic effects of the uterine horns indicate that the luteolytic activity of the right horn is more localized, while the activity of the left one is both systematic and local (Fernández-Baca *et al* 1979).

Birth in alpacas only occur during the early hours of the day. No births occur between 17.00 and 04.00, a time when temperatures are low throughout the year in Peru (Sumar, 1983). The time for 93.5% of births was between 07.00 and 13.00 h, which shows an admirable adaptation of these animals to the Andean environment, where even in the summer, temperatures below zero are common. This is also in contrast with what happens with the time of parturition in ewes in the highlands of Peru, where the majority of births occur during the hours of darkness. Another peculiarity of the alpaca at birth is that they do not lick their offspring or eat the placenta. Alpacas and llamas are excellent mothers, and rarely abandon their offspring, even given a poor nutritional status.

Postpartum period
Up to the fourth day after parturition, the female alpaca is submissive and can be mounted by the male. However, she is not fertile, since the regression of the corpus luteum, follicular growth and the involution of the uterus, are pre-requisites to renewed sexual activity. Five days after giving birth, some females show acceptance of the males, and if copulation occurs, occasional ovulation and fertilization occur. Ten days postpartum the follicles are 8-10 mm in size, the corpus luteum has regressed considerably, and the uterus involuted, weighing only a fifth of its weight 24 hours after birth. Servicing of the females is recommended within 15-20 days of them giving birth in order to obtain good fertility results (Sumar *et al* 1972).

The Placenta
The placenta in the alpaca, as in other camelids, is diffuse and epiteliochorial in type. The chorionic epithelium is thrown into unbranched villi or folds, which are closely opposed to corresponding undulations of the uterine ephitelium, and the fetal-maternal interface consists of an intricate interdigitation of fetal and maternal microvilli. In late gestation both chorionic and uterine epithelia are deeply indented by placental capillaries, so

that the minimum intercapillary distance across the diffusion pathway may be as little as 2 μm. This distance appears to be less than that found in the epithelio-chorial placenta of any other species of domestic ungulates in late gestation and may be one of the several adaptations to pregnancy at high altitude (Stevens *et al* 1980). Delivery of the fetal membranes occurs some 45 minutes after the birth of the fetus.

Artificial Insemination

A number of studies have been made on the feasibility of artificial insemination in alpacas and llamas. Inter-species crosses have also been tested between alpaca and vicuña (the F1 is known as the paco-vicuña) and between vicuña and llama (llama-Vicuña). Calderón *et al* (1968) conducted a study to determine the most appropriate time for insemination after ovulation had been induced with vasectomized males and with hCG. They found that the highest proportion of fertilized ova occurred between 35-45 hours following induced ovulation. The fertility rates were higher using vasectomized males to induce ovulation than when using hCG. Also, in this study, insemination was performed during the recto-palpation method, depositing the semen in the horns of the uterus.

It is necessary to note that the South American camelids offer advantages over other species in the use of artificial insemination. Since females are in continuous oestrus during the breeding season, ovulation can be induced with a vasectomized male, and the insemination can be intrauterine, in the left uterine horn, since 98.5% of implantations occurred in this horn. Still, the birth rates are low due to the failure of the females to ovulate, to embryo mortality or other factors. It is interesting to note that under conditions of natural mating with only one service, the birth rates are also low (Sumar, unpublished data).

Embryo transfer

Novoa and Sumar (1968) reported for the first time the collection of ova after induced ovulation as well as after superovulation. The ova were collected by surgery and flushing took place from the oviduct towards the horn of the uterus, as it is impossible to pass fluids from the uterus to the oviduct due to a papilla in the utero-tubal junction. This procedure yielded a mean of three eggs per collection while the number of corpora lutea was six on average. Subsequently, embryo transfer was tried in alpacas (Sumar and Franco, 1974) using 44 receptors and 15 donors. The eggs were collected surgically and were transferred to the receptors. Four females became pregnant. The poor results were partly due to difficulties to get a suitable medium for transfer or indeed to other functional requirements. There is a report from USA, about non-surgical embryo transfer, where two donor female llamas were flushed non-surgically and one viable 7-day-old embryo was recovered and transferred non-surgically within four hours into a recipient female llama whose oestrus was synchronized with the donor by injection of GnRH. A normal and healthy male was born, 326 days following transfer (Wiepz and Chapman, 1985).

FINAL REMARKS

South American domestic camelids production is an important activity for many inhabitants of the high Andes, which offer very few other alternatives for livelihood due to the ecological limitations of the region and to economic constraints.

The existing management systems are extrapolations of those techniques developed for other species, particularly sheep, although it is now very well established that the physiological characteristics of camelids are significantly different to those of sheep. The need for developing knowledge of camelids physiology and management is thus apparent.

One of the major breeding problems is inbreeding. Due to the lack of new breeding lines, the inbreeding problem is undoubtedly an important cause of the high incidence of genetic abnormalities. Therefore, proper attention should be given to this aspect and exchange of breeding males should be encouraged.

Since the bulk of the alpaca and llama population in all the Andean countries are owned by the highland peasants and they are the poorest inhabitants of this region, special emphasis must be placed on extension programmes. The initiation of social and economic research before or at the same time as biological research, can reduce the probability of undesirable effects on the introduction of improved technology. Thus, any research with the objective of improving camelids production in the high Andean region must be multi-disciplinary.

REFERENCES

Benirschke, K. 1967: "Sterility and Fertility of Interspecific Mammalian Hybrids", in: *Comparative Aspects of Reproductive Failures.* New York: Spring Verlag.

Bunch, T.D. and Foote, W.C. 1983: "Chromosome banding pattern relationship of the Llama *(Lama glama)* and the Bactrian camel *(Camelus bactrianus)"*. *ADSA Annual Meeting and Divisional Abstracts,* Supplement 1. JDS, Volume 66. University of Wisconsin.

Calderón, W., Sumar, J. and Franco, E. 1968: "Avances en la Inseminación Artificial de las Alpacas *(Lama pacos)"*, in: *Revista de la Facultad de Medicina Veterinaria,* Vol 22, 19. Lima, Peru: Universidad Nacional Mayor de San Marcos.

Chen, B.X., Yuen, Z.X. and Pan G.W. 1985: "Semen induced ovulation in the Bactrian camel *(Camelus bactrianus)"*, in: *J. Reprod. Fertil.,* 74: 335-339.

Engelhardt, W. von, Rubsamen, K. and Heller, R. 1984: "The Digestive Physiology of Camelids", in: *The Camelid: an all-purpose animal*. Proceedings of the Khartoum Workshop on Camels. December 1979. Uppsala: Scandinavian Institute of African Studies.

Fernández-Baca, S. and Calderón, W. 1966: "Métodos de Coleción de Semen de la Alpaca", in: *Revista de la Facultad de Medicina Veterinaria*. Vol 18-20, 13. Lima, Peru: Universidad Nacional Mayor de San Marcos.

Fernández-Baca, S., Hansel W. and Novoa C. 1970: "Embryonic Mortality in the Alpaca", in: *Biol. Reprod.*, 3, 243-251.

Fernández-Baca, S., Sumar J. and Novoa C. 1972: "Comportamiento Sexual de la Alpaca Macho, Frente a la Renovación de las Hembras", in: *Rev. Inv. Pec.*, 1(12): 115-128. Julio/diciembre. IVITA, Universidad Nacional Mayor de San Marcos.

Fernández-Baca, S., Sumar J. and Novoa C. and Leyva, V. 1973: "Relación entre la Ubicación del Cuerpo Luteo y la Localización del Embrión en la Alpaca", in: *Rev. Inv. Pec.*, 2, 131-135. IVITA, Universidad Nacional Mayor de San Marcos.

Fernández-Baca, S., Hansel, W., Saatman, R., Sumar, J. and Novoa, C. 1979: "Differential Luteolytic Effect on Right and Left Uterine Horns in the Alpaca", in: *Biol. Reprod.*, 20, 586-595.

Flores-Ochoa, J. A. 1977: "Pastores de Alpacas de Los Andes", in J.A. Flores-Ochoa (ed): *Pastores de Puna*, pp 15-22. Lima, Peru: Instituto de Estudios Andinos.

Franklin, W. L. 1978: *Socioecology of the Vicuña*. Ann Arbor: University Microfilm International.

Koford, C. B. 1957: "The Vicuña and the Puna", in: *Ecol. Monog.*, 27, 153.

Kubiceck, J. von 1974: "Samanentnahme beim Alpaka durch eine Harnrohrenfistel", in: *Z. Tierzuch. Zuchtgsbiol.*, 90, 335-351.

Leyva, V. and Sumar, J. 1981: *Evaluación del Peso Corporal al Empadre Sobre la Capacidad Reproductiva de Hembras Alpaca de Un Año de Edad IV Convención Nacional forestal e Instituto de la Patagonia*. 22-27 noviembre. Punta Arenas, Chile.

Mogrovejo, D. 1952: *Estudios del Semen de la Alpaca*. Tesis de Bachiller. Lima, Peru: Facultad de Medicina Veterinaria, Universidad Nacional Mayor de San Marcos.

Novoa, C. and Sumar, J. 1968: "Colección de Huevos *in vivo* y Ensayo de Transferencia de embriones en Alpacas", in: *Tercer Boletin Extraordinario*. Lima, Peru: IVITA, Universidad Nacional Mayor de San Marcos, .

Novoa, C. and Sumar, J. and Franco, E. 1970: "Empadre Complementario de Hembres Alpaca Vacías", in: *Cuarto Boletin Extraordinario*, Lima, Peru: IVITA, Universidad Nacional Mayor de San Marcos.

Orlove, B. 1980: "Pastoralism in the Southern Sierra", in: *Andean Peasant Economics and Pastoralism*. Publication 1. Columbia: Small Ruminant CRSP, Department of Rural Sociology, University of Missouri.

Rios, M., Sumar, J. and Ararcón, V. 1985: "Presencia de un Factor de Inducción de la Ovulación en el Semen de la Alpaca y Toro". *VIII Reunión Anual de la Asociación Peruana de Producción Animal* (APPA), Huancayo, Peru.

San Martin, M., Copaira, M., Zuñiga, J., Rodriguez, R., Bustinza, G. and Acosta, L. 1968: "Aspects of Reproduction in the Alpaca", in: *J. Reprod. Fertil.*, 16, 395-399.

Sumar, J. 1980: "Gestación Gemelar en la Alpaca", in: *Rev. Inv. Pec.*, 5(1): 58-60. IVITA, Universidad Nacional Mayor de San Marcos.

Sumar, J. 1983: *Studies on Reproductive Pathology: With a Review of Normal Reproductive Anatomy and Physiology*. MVSc Thesis. Uppsala: Faculty of Veterinary Medicine, Swedish University of Agricultural Sciences.

Sumar, J. and Bravo, W. 1981: "Efecto Endocrino Fisiológico del Receptal en Alpacas". *IV Convención Internacional sobre Camélidos Sudamericanos*. 22-27 noviembre. Corporación Nacional Forestal e Instituto de la Patagonia. Punta Arenas, Chile.

Sumar, J. and Bravo, W. 1982: "Corpus Luteum Function in the Maintenance of Pregnancy in the Llama", in: *FAO/SIDA Follow-up Seminar on Animal Reproduction*. Volume II. Lima, Peru.

Sumar, J. and Bravo, W. 1982a: "Relación entre Intensidad de Celo, Ocurrencia y Tiempo de Ovulación y Sobrevivencia Embrionaria en Alpacas", in: *Investigaciones en Camélidos Sudamericanos y en Ovinos*. Programa Colaborativo de Investigación en Pequeños Rumiantes (SR-CRSP). Título XII-AID. Período 1980-1984. Lima, Peru: IVITA, Universidad Nacional Mayor de San Marcos.

Sumar, J. and Garcia, M. 1986: "Fisiología de la Reproducción de la Alpaca", in: *Nuclear and Related Techniques in Animal Production and Health*. Proceeding of a Symposium, Vienna, jointly organized by IAEA and FAO. Vienna: International Atomic Energy Agency.

Sumar, J. and Franco, E. 1974: "Ensayos de Transferencia de Embriones en Camélidos Sudamericanos", in: *Informe Final*. Lima, Peru: IVITA, Universidad Nacional Mayor de San Marcos.

Sumar, J. and Leyva, V. 1981: "Colección de Semen Mediante Vagina Artificial en la Alpaca *(Lama pacos)*." *IV Convención Internacional sobre Camélidos Sudamericanos*. 22-27 noviembre. Corporación Nacional Forestal e Instituto de la Patagonia. Punta Arenas, Chile.

Sumar, J. and Leyva, V. 1981a: "Rol del Cuerpo Luteo en el Mantenimiento de la Preñez en la Alpaca *(Lama pacos)*". *IV Convención Internacional sobre Camélidos Sudamericanos*. 22-27 noviembre. Corporación Nacional Forestal e Instituto de la Patagonia. Punta Arenas, Chile.

Sumar, J, Novoa, C. and Fernández-Baca, S. 1972: "Fisiología Reproductiva Post-partum en la Alpaca", in: *Rev. Inv. Pec.*, 1:21-27. IVITA, Universidad Nacional Mayor de San Marcos.

Stevens, D.H., Burton, G.J., Sumar, J. and Nathanielsz, P. W. 1980: "Ultrastructural Observations of the Placenta of the Alpaca *(Lama pacos)*", in: *Placenta*, 1, 21-32.

Taylor, K.M., Hungerford, D.A., Snyder R.L. and Umer, F.A. Jr. 1968: "Uniformity of Karyotypes in the *Camelidae*", in: *Cytogenetics*, 7:7.

Tosi, J.A. 1960: "Zonas de Vida Natural en el Peru", in: *Publ. Boletin Técnico*, No 5. Lima, Peru: IICA.

Wiepz, D.W. and Chapman, R.J. 1985: "Non-surgical Embryo Transfer and Live Birth in a Llama", in L.W. Johnson (ed): *Llama Medicine Workshop for Veterinarians*. Fort Collins: College of Veterinary Medicine and Biomedical Sciences, Colorado State University.

TABLE

Table 1. *Estimated number of South American camelids*

Country	Alpaca	Llama	Guanaco	Vicuña	Total	Percent within each country
Peru	2,490,000 (88,9%)	1,361,050 (37,9%)	5,000 (0,9%)	65,000 (72,6%)	3,921,050	55,6%
Bolivia	300,000 (10,71%)	2,050,000 (57,0%)	Few	4,500 (5,0%)	2,354,500	33,4%
Argentina	Few	100,000	550,000	10,000	660,000	9,4%
Chile	10,000	75,000	20,000	10,000	115,000	1,5%
Ecuador	Few	2,500	...	...	2,500	0,03%
USA	500	5,000	Few	...	5,500	0,07%
Total	2,800,500	3,593,550	575,000	89,500	7,058,550	
Percent of total camelids	39,7%	50,9%	8,1%	1,3%	...	100%

DISCUSSANT'S REPORT

N Shanmugaratnam

Highlights of the discussion

a) The importance of Research
There was consensus on the need for further research on various aspects of camel pastoralism as a production system with the view to identify sustainable alternatives. This production system has been under growing pressure from forces emanating mainly from the large socio-political environment. Moreover, in most countries concerned national policies have tended to undervalue the potentials of camel pastoralism and neglect the well-being of the people engaged in it. All this has contributed to the increased vulnerability of the production system to environmental stress and perturbation.

In such an overall context of neglect of camel pastoralism, the establishment of a national research centre for camel development in India - which has only 6.3% of the world's camels - stands out as a unique case of recognition of camel pastoralism as a production system with a future. About 75% of the world's camel population is found in Africa, with the bulk of it in East Africa. Many speakers strongly favoured the establishment of an African research centre to carry out sustained collaborative studies.

Available research findings clearly showed that camels are not only ideally suited for the ecological conditions or arid and semi-arid regions but are also of great economic value in terms of milk, meat, wool and draught power. However, further work is needed to find ways of improving the production system as a whole.

b) Integrated/holistic approaches

While discussing Dr Khanna's and Dr Sumar's papers the group returned, though briefly, to the framework presented by Dr Hjort the previous day. In his paper, Dr Hjort argued for a holistic approach that addressed the key issues concerning the future of camel pastoralism, including reproduction of family herds. Some participants sought to articulate research needs from the perspective that informed Hjort's paper. The biological properties of camelids concerning adaptability to arid conditions; quantity and quality of camel products; population dynamics; and draught power - all had to be seen in a holistic perspective that treated camel pastoralism as a production system in need of qualitative improvements to suit changing social conditions. Although this was well recognized by everyone the discussion remained incomplete, mainly due to lack of time.

c) South-south collaboration

There was a general consensus that effective channels of communication should be created between scientific workers in Africa, Asia and Latin America on camel pastoral development. The absence of a regional research institution dealing with camel development in Africa is a major obstacle to the institutionalization of such relations. ILCA has not been able to promote South-South links in a sustained manner on this subject because of its changing research priorities.

The Case of African Drylands and Balanced Camel Production

A veterinary point of view

Set Bornstein

A broad multidisciplinary approach has to be taken when discussing camel production in the drylands of Africa or, for that matter, any production for food that can be produced from available biomass.

The world at large has become aware of the ecological disasters threatening many areas of the world, be it the devastated rainforests or the large tracts of arid areas, where existence for humans and animals is threatened over and over again.

Africa, particularly the Sahel, has been in the limelight during the last one and a half decades. Natural causes like annual droughts, coupled with misapplied or misdirected measures, have had catastrophic results. To stop the spread of the deserts and to make the soil fertile again is of vital importance for all of us.

In this context the camel has a very special place - being highly adaptive to hot and arid conditions and an excellent producer of milk, meat and wool fibres. It can stand this harsh environment better than any other domestic animal.

In some development projects concerned with livestock promotion in the Sahelian and Sudan-Sahelian zones, camels are never considered, nor even mentioned in background papers and studies describing the country and project area. This gives the impression that none of the experts (local or expatriates) have visited the area or even been informed about the existence here of camels (e.g. Niger[*], Wardle 1979 in *Pastoral Network Paper*, 8c).

The camel population has decreased in some countries this century (e.g. in the Mahgreb countries), while in others it has increased. As a result of increased understanding of the fantastic capabilities of the camel, a new interest in promoting camel husbandry is on its way both in countries such as Sudan and Somalia that have recognized the importance of the animal, as well as in those countries (e.g. Niger) which once had larger herds (Richard et al. 1985 IEMVT).

---

[*] This is, however, being rectified. See "Projet de Developpement de l'elevage dans le Niger Centre-Est". Productions Cameline: D. Richard, D. Planchenault and J.F. Giovannetti 1985, IEMVT.

Africa has a substantial number of the world's dromedary camels (Camelus dromedarius); 80%, or 12-13 million, in over 18 countries on the continent (not including recent introduction to Botswana, Namibia and the Canary Islands).

Those countries with the highest camel population are Somalia, with over 5 million, followed by Sudan, with 3 million, which together account for more than 70% of all camels on the African continent. Ethiopia, Kenya and Chad account for another 12-13%. Mauretania, Niger and Mali also have substantial numbers as have some of the Mahgreb countries.

IMPORTANCE IN RELATION TO DOMESTIC HERBIVORE BIOMASS

There is an interesting measurement that indicates the importance of camels in relation to other livestock; camels as a percentage of the domestic herbivore biomass, DHB (Wilson, 1984). Wilson groups the countries with camel populations into 4 categories: Category 1 are countries whose camels contribute less than 1% total DHB. In Africa, Nigeria, Senegal and Burkina Faso belong to this category. In all these countries cattle are equivalent to about 75% DHB. In Category 2 camels contribute 1-8% of the total DHB. Seven countries in Africa belong in this group: Egypt, Ethiopia, Morocco, Mali, Algeria, Kenya, and Libya. Within these countries there are individual households for which camels are the most important livestock. Category 3 is composed of countries where camels have 8-20% of DHB. In Africa, according to Wilson, these countries are Niger, Chad, Tunisia, and Sudan. In Category 4 belong four African countries where camels constitute more than 20% of DHB: Mauretania, Djibouti, Somalia, and Western Sahara. These countries contain about 40% of the world's dromedary camel population.

One could perhaps come to even higher figures showing the relative importance of the camel if milk output per female camel was compared to that of cattle, sheep or goats.

We know that camels feeding on the same pasture as cattle, sheep and goats, will produce much more milk and continue to produce even throughout dry seasons. Their lactation periods (6-18 months) can thus extend well into several dry seasons.

Spencer (1973) found that during the dry season one Rendille camel produces as much milk as 4 Samburu (zebu) cows during the rainy season.

The milk yields of different breeds of camel vary in different areas of the world, from a little over 1,000 kgs to over 12,000 kgs per lactation period (Knoess 1979, Wilson 1984). Animals with an alleged yield of over 2-3,000 kgs per lactation period are presumably kept and managed more intensively (as in Pakistan or USSR) than in Africa.

THE POTENTIAL

Many people (Somalis, Rendille etc) who have managed their herds extensively on ranges have kept camels mainly for milk and have bred them for
the same purpose. However, there is still presumably a potential to increase their production capacity (by "scientific breeding").

Even so, yields can be increased only if the animals' management is improved, particularly as concerns of feeding and veterinary services. Knoess
(1977) kept the small and slender Afar camels (Ethiopia) from pastoralist
herds on alfa-alfa and Panicum maximum - cultivated on irrigated pastures. These extremely well-fed animals yielded over 2,800 kgs of milk per
14 months lactation period.

In certain suitable areas around towns and other urban centres where
the demand for milk is high, camel dairy farms and dairies could be set up.

MEAT PRODUCTION

The meat yield is not to be neglected. There is a demand, and seemingly a
growing demand, for camel meat in camel-breeding societies in Africa as
well as in Arab countries (Bremaud 1969). Large numbers of camels are
trekked from Subsaharan countries to the Arab countries in North Africa
(Swift 1979). Quite a number are exported on ships alive to the Middle East
for slaughter. Saudi Arabia and some of the Gulf states are importing riding camels for pleasure and racing; these are supplied in particular by Sudan. Niger and Egypt import camels for food (Alim 1976).

Amongst the camel-herding societies camel meat is usually highly appreciated. However, as a rule camels are only slaughtered on very special
occasions; unless too old or diseased they are too valuable to be slaughtered. There is often a legal prohibition against slaughtering healthy adult
female camels if not too old or infertile. In some societies, most male calves
are killed at an early age so as to save milk for human consumption, particularly if there is no need for castrated baggage animals.

WOOL, HAIR AND HIDES

Camel wool, hair and hides should not be overlooked.

Wool is an important product of the Bactrian camel though it can also be
obtained from the dromedary camel. More hair is found on animals in
cooler climates, while the best hair comes from young camels. In Saudi
Arabia the average amount expected from a camel is 1-2 kilo per season

(Dorman 1984), in the Sudan 0.5-1.5 kilo annually (El Amin 1979). Tents, rugs, clothing and bedouin cloaks are manufactured from camel hair.

HIDES

Well-prepared good quality camel hides could be attractive to the leather industry (Ibrahim and Abu-Samra 1987), but most hides coming from Africa are of bad quality, for several reasons: disease and ectoparasites, branding of the skin, (a common practice in disease treatment and in marking the ownership), methods of skinning after slaughter and, to some extent, the local drying procedure. However, camel leather is used in making sandals, bags, whips and other household products and in the Mahgreb countries, tourist items like seat-cushions, saddles etc.

TRANSPORT

Most societies that have camels use them not only for food, but also as work animals: in Africa as baggage and riding animals and to a lesser extent for cultivation, drawing water and milling (for meal and oil production). Camels in some Asian countries are often seen before the plough or pulling carts.

Thousands of camels are bred every year only for sports and many of these are exported (e.g. from the Sudan).

OPTIMUM UTILIZATION

The carrying capacity for camels on different types of range and under different types of climate has not been studied. Nor has the optimum multi-livestock stocking rate (i.e. mixed species such as camels with cattle and/or sheep or goats or with donkeys).

Some ranches in Kenya have recently introduced herds of camels onto rangelands traditionally devoted to cattle, sheep and goats with promising results. Camels have improved the pastures by opening up the bush for the other domestic species and achieving better bush control (Evans and Powys 1984). The camels browse on a variety of species of shrubs and trees that the other animals avoid or cannot reach, thus increasing the productivity of the land without really competing with them for food.

VETERINARY ASPECTS

Although the camel is a hard and tough beast it is prone to disease like any other species. In general, little research has been made on the camel since the First World War.

However, there are a few important known diseases affecting camels in particular, e.g. Surra or Camel trypanosomiasis, Camel pox, Sarcoptic mange, gastrointestinal diseases caused by helminths like the gutworm Haemonchus sp or bacteria like Salmonella spp, Clostridium spp. There are also respiratory diseases caused by viruses and bacteria like haemorrhagic septicaemia (HS).

Some of the diseases that camels encounter may be found only in these animals, e.g. Camel pox. Others, however, affect other livestock and game animals, e.g. sarcoptic mange, HS, hydatid disease. Others again, are zoonotic diseases, i.e. they can also affect man; e.g. hydatid disease, salmonellosis, tuberculosis, brucellosis, anthrax etc.

The most common known diseases of camels can be treated and prophylactically covered (e.g. drenches of anthelmintics, acaricides, trypanocidal drugs, vaccinations).

It has been shown in Kenya (Rutagwenda 1984) that by giving regularly a simple veterinary drug package against the most important pathogens (disease agents) the number of animals in a treated herd was increased by 18% in one year. A net loss of 5% of the animals that year was encountered in the untreated (control) herd.

We know that calf mortality is very high, with up to 40% deaths not uncommon (Richard et al. 1985).

With veterinary service and better management the very high calf mortality can be reduced considerably. Rutagwenda (1984) confirmed that, for example, malnutrition in camel calves was a problem in Northern Kenya partly due to competition between humans and calves for the milk. Richard et al. (1985) report the same from Niger.

HARMFUL MANAGEMENT

Management practices can be harmful. In some societies the colostrum is not given immediately or at all to the newborn camel calf, which thus is deprived of its mother's antibodies as a protection against the pathogens in the environment which can threaten the life of the calf.

Rather small but consistent measures could prevent disease and the death of the young. They could also prevent subclinical disease, which can cause reduced growth rate.

SLOW GROWTH RATE OF HERDS

Many scientists who are concerned with camel pastoralism are worried about the slow reproductive performance of camels, compared to that of cattle and small stock. Camels are pregnant about 12 months and will reproduce every 2-3 years, so the pastoralists' herds grow quite slowly. It takes some years to build up a "family" camel herd again after a severe drought or other major disaster (Dahl and Hjort 1976). Yagil and Etsion (1984) have shown that one can increase the reproductive rate by at least 100%. A fertile, healthy and well-fed camel should be able to calve at least every 18 months. But, irrespective of the slow reproductive rate of camels reared extensively in Africa, better management and disease control would increase camel numbers considerably.

FEEDING AND FODDER

Camels have a great advantage over most other domestic herbivores in that they are mainly browsers. They so reach higher up in the canopy of trees and bushes than most other animals, and thus compete very little with other livestock.

They eat a variety of plants, bushes, leaves and twigs of trees and their pods - some of which other livestock do not eat.

A characteristic of camels' food habits is their craving for salt, which they must regularly consume in order to function properly. It has to do with their special physiological set up - kidney function and water regulation - so well adapted to a life in the hot and arid lands.

The camels' craving for salt is well known. The animals are regularly taken to salty pastures, salty waters or soils containing salt (NaCl). There are quite a few plants and bushes that contain high amounts of salt, e.g. Atriplex spp. These are usually rich in protein and water.

Many of these species of bushes and trees from different areas of the world are being studied for their ability to grow in salty soil and in very hot and arid environments. A variety of species of trees and bushes, which are able to establish themselves and survive in arid environments, are being tested (Zohar et al. 1986).

RE-ESTABLISHING THE RANGE

Drought-resistant fodder shrubs and trees under rainfed conditions could and should be planted on depleted ranges to stop the erosion and desertification process. Such plants would supply livestock (not only camels) with fodder and humans with firewood and would help in refertilizing the environment.

From the beginning trees have been man's blessing. Trees give pleasure, beauty, shade, tranquillity and coolness, and they clear the air of dust. The power of the winds is reduced in strength by up to 50%. Great numbers will stop the ever increasing and encroaching sand dunes.

Trees produce oxygen for the benefit of vegetation, of animals and of human beings. Through the roots the groundwater will rise. There are species of trees planted today in these deserts whose roots reach 100 metres deep. The composition of the soil is affected by trees in such a way that other vegetation may be established and grow. The whole micro-climate as well as the macro-climate are changed. Trees increase the moistness of the air, increasing the possibilities for vegetation to be established and to flourish.

A number of tree species give food for humans and animals. Many are rich producers of fodder and give protein-rich foods.

All development projects in dry lands should have a component of reforestation to stop desert encroachment, to supply us with fodder and food, firewood and building material. Trees will give us back the beauty and tranquillity of the landscape, a sounder ecology.

Reforestation programmes are particularly relevant to camel husbandry given that animal's preferences for browsing a wide range of hardy, heat- and drought-resistant plants (bushes, trees and various pods).

CONCLUSIONS

Camels are under-exploited in African dry lands. There is presumably a big potential for increasing numbers of camels (as well as restocking) in areas where camels are husbanded and to introduce them into new areas; improving camel management by people who raise camels extensively (nomadism and ranching) and intensively (fattening and dairy farm development) and as a multipurpose animal for work and recreation. The camel competes well with oxen, mules, donkeys and horses.

Even if genetically yields can be increased, camels cannot give more milk without improved management, particularly better nutrition and veterinary services.

Projects in these fields must be coupled with research. However, today we know enough to start small-scale projects - but these have to be accurately managed and scientifically monitored.

Little attention has been paid to the study of camels. There are vast gaps in our knowledge in camel physiology, behaviour, and so on. Interdisciplinary discussions and studies, including research into social, cultural and economic problems in camel husbandry, must involve the participation of the people concerned before implementing any "development" project; respect of Man and the environment is paramount.

REFERENCES

Dahl, G. and Hjort, A. 1976: *Having herds: Pastoral herd growth and household economy*, University of Stockholm.

Dorman, A.E., 1984: "Two aspects of the husbandry and management of the genus Camelus", in: *British Veterinary Journal*, 140, 616.

El Amin, F.M., 1984: "The dromedary of the Sudan", in: *The camelid - an all-purpose animal*. Vol 1, Proceedings from the Khartoum Workshop on Camels, 1979. Uppsala: Scandinavian Institute of African Studies.

Evans, J.O. and Powys, J.G., 1984: "Camel husbandry in Kenya: Increasing the productivity of ranch lands", in: *The camelid - an all-purpose animal*. Vol 1, Proceedings from the Khartoum Workshop on Camels, 1979. Uppsala: Scandinavian Institute of African Studies.

Ibrahim, K.E.E., and Abu-Samra, M.T. 1987: "Crust leather prepared from the hide of the one-humped camel (Camelus Dromedarius)", in: *Annual Report, Camel Research Project, May 1987*. Sudan: National Council for Research.

Knoess, K.H., 1984: "The camel as a meat and milk animal", in: *World Animal Review*, 223, 3-8.

Knoess, K.H., 1984: "The milk dromedary", in: *The camelid - an all-purpose animal*. Vol 1, Proceedings from the Khartoum Workshop on Camels, 1979. Uppsala: Scandinavian Institute of African Studies.

Richard, D., 1984: *Le dromedaire et son élevage*. IEMVT, 1985. Institut d'élevage et de médicine vétérinaire des pays tropicaux.

Rutagwenda, R., 1984: "The state of knowledge on camel diseases in Northern Kenya". *Camel pastoralism seminar in Marsabit*, 1984.

Spencer, P. 1973: *Nomads in alliance: Symbiosis and growth among the Rendille and Samburu of Kenya*. Oxford University Press.

Wilson, R.T., 1984: *The Camel*. London and New York: Longman.

Yagil, R., 1984: "The adaptation of domesticated animals to arid zones with special reference to the camel", in: *Refuah Veterinarith*, 41(4), 144-156.

Zohar, Y., Lovenstein, H. and Aronso, 1987: "Food, fodder and firewood. Cultivation under water-harvesting systems in the arid regions of Israel". *Second International Conference on desert development*, January 1987. Cairo.

Camel Herd Dynamics in Southern Somalia: Long Term Development and Milk Production Implications[1]

Mohamed Ali Hussein
Anders Hjort af Ornäs

The last ten or 15 years have seen a bandwagon effect in the study of dryland problems; and much has been written about the critical situation in Africa, not least in the drylands. But limited insights into what kinds of issues need to be studied have led to a rather fragmented picture. Many have studied similar problem areas whereas some issues have not been touched upon at all. When it comes to the study of pastoral systems there are severe knowledge gaps due to the different perspectives of the natural and social sciences as well as the practical difficulties of carrying out long-term research in hot and dry climates.

The prevailing ecological situation is based on balances or imbalances between its three components: people, animals and land (Hjort 1981). What are lacking, generally speaking, are detailed insights, for instance into age structures of pastoral herds, decision-making and competence levels, how plants are differentiated depending on their use as fodder and the implications of seasonality (see Hjort 1985 for further discussions on this point).

This kind of knowledge gap also exist in the Somali context. There is, for instance, no information on the composition of family herds of camels detailed enough to allow for any "demographical" calculations of long-term developments. With the present essay we want to test to what extent such problems can be overcome by means of aerial surveying.

CAMEL HERD DYNAMICS

This article derives from work within the Somali Camel Research Project and is based particularly on an aerial survey proposed by R. M. Watson (1986) and on ground surveying by Mohamed Ali Hussein. These surveys were carried out in mid-1984. Our prime concern is to analyse camel herd compositions in southern Somalia presented in Watson (ibid) by looking at long-term implications in terms of herd growth and at milk production

---

[1] This is a revised version of a working paper in the *Camel Forum* series, published at the Scandinavian Institute of African Studies.

possibilities in eleven selected camel herds. These herds contained in all 4,454 camels. The locations of the herds surveyed are given on Map I.

The results of the aerial survey combined with data from the ground survey to a correlation curve between age (up to ten years) and size. The ground survey also creates the possibility of establishing sex. This means that the method is but a partial way of solving the problem of age distributions. We even doubt whether it is efficient up to ten years; the slope in the correlation curve tends towards 0 already at the age of eight. Here we do not utilize findings beyond the age class 7-8 years.

The data from the section on herd composition is accordingly not comprehensive for the discussion on long-term growth in family herds. In the following section we have therefore been forced to estimate age distributions above the age of 10 and until 22 (when we have assumed animals to be slaughtered). The estimations made derive from extensive reading of the literature. Since we simulate herd growth over a long period of time, the reproduction behaviour will eventually generate a typical herd structure.

In terms of possible milk production from the family herds the data on herd composition are more reliable, granted that proper herd management leads to a decision to keep only those adult females which can safely be assumed to be fertile. That section draws conclusions about the size of herd required by a household dependent on the herd for its food supply.

The concluding section draws on (i) the fact that milk is a staple of food (at least ideally) in this part of Somalia; (ii) that camel husbandry often has to be combined with other activities; and (iii) that family herds have typical profiles, such as pre-drought and post-drought characters.

HERD COMPOSITION

The age and sex composition of the eleven herds surveyed is given in Table I. The same table is summarized later in Table VII.

There are a few points about Table I which can be immediately observed. To begin with, we see more females than males already in the age interval 1/2-1. The reason is a herd management practice which gives preference to females; male calves are to a considerable extent slaughtered at birth. Since calf mortalities are high (Williamson and Payne 1965:298) it is considered preferable to slaughter surviving males rather than risk the whole calf population.

The ratio of mature males in the herds is slightly below 1:10. These animals may be used both for transport and reproduction. Normally, remaining males are castrated at the age of 4-6 years (Mares 1954:418) in order to improve handling. The number of bulls needed for reproduction is small. One male can serve at least 30 females and many sources have it that he may serve as many as 100 females (see Dahl and Hjort 1976:78f). This is also in accordance with what herdsmen claim.

From the table one can plot the proportion of females per one-year interval. We have done so until the interval 7-8 years. Average proportions per age interval are presented Table II.

In Table II we have distributed remaining animals evenly; that is, a proportion of 1.5% of the total herd per age class from 8-9 until 18-19. The last two age-classes in the table, however, have been somewhat diminished, representing only 1.0% each of the total herd. We assume that no animals live after the age of 21 years; they are presumed to be slaughtered at 21. We rely in this assumption not only on Mares (1954:417f) but also on our own empirical impressions.

LONG-TERM PROJECTIONS

Table II is the point of departure for long-term simulations. As we have already mentioned, the empirical distribution after the age of eight is a little bit uncertain, but this is not, however, detrimental for the projections. What are decisive over time are calving rates and the total number of fertile females.

Departing from Mares (1954:417), Dahl and Hjort (1976) discuss annual calving rates and conclude: one of 0.25 calves per fertile female and year. This means one birth strictly every other year for the "statistical female" and an exact 1:1 ratio between female and male calves. Data from the eleven surveyed herds reveal the ratios in Table III.

Looking at the table, we see that different categories of family camel herds are represented. Herd number 2 is made up of extremely young animals. Herds 8 and 9 consist of extremely few young ones. Projections for any one of these herds will lead to a population boom and extinction respectively. There might be several reasons for the presence of such herds; they could be dry and milk herds, or post- and predrought herds.

Our conclusion for long-term development is that the average calving rate is 0.37. This rate is quite high. It implies a development towards young camel herds in comparison with what can be anticipated for other parts of Africa. The rate is also higher than what Watson (1986:11) has noted for northern Kenya.

Crucial for the projection is also what mortality rates we assume. Calf mortality is extremely high for camels: Dahl and Hjort (1976:82) give a figure of 30%. In our case we can but calculate a rough mortality distribution according to age distributions. This is done in Table IV, where also the figures are rounded so as to be better suited for a model.

The distribution is but a rough estimate. "The model" column is formed through a combination of the assumptions by Dahl and Hjort (1976:83) in one of their cases, and a calculation from the survey data. The latter calculation is a treatment of the age-classes as if they were made up of the same animals over a sequence of years. This assumption is naturally not quite true, as is evidenced by a few anomalies that appear in the table (survival rates above 100%). In the model, animals in age-class n+1 are seen as the survivors from age-class n. With this rather crude approach due to limited data we cannot account for annual fluctuations.

We see that few animals survived the interval 7-8 years before the survey, i.e. 1976/77. The empirical evidence is that a drought occurred a year before. In the model we leave the guidance of the survey data at that point and follow Dahl's and Hjort's assumptions. Calf mortality in the is model assumed to be 30% and the animals are presumed to die after the age of 21.

With these assumptions we can follow the algorithm presented by Dahl and Hjort (1976:49) for herd growth in southern Somalia. The number of female camels, n, in the age interval (i,i+1) at t years after a change has occurred, is:

$$\text{For } i=0,\ n_{i,t}= \sum_{k=4}^{21} f_{k,t-1}$$

$$\text{For } 1 \leq i \leq 21,\ n_{i,t}=(1-d_i){*}n_{i-1,t-1}$$

Here d_i is the relative number of individual camels in the age interval (i-1) that die at this age, and f_i is the relative number of females in the age interval (i,i+1) that give birth to female calves. The class boundary in the algorithm is set at the upper age in the interval. This modelling assumes that all animals remain alive until they are to shift up to the higher age-class. At this point all doomed to death in the model during the year are assumed dying. Variations, for instance in fodder intake, have to be assumed as integrated in mortality figures.

Figures I and II present the results in comparison with the second case of Dahl and Hjort. The data behind is presented in our working paper, see footnote 1, in pp. 13-14.

We see that the emerging annual growth rate in the case of southern Somalia tends towards 4.9%, whereas it is around 1.5% in the theoretical case of Dahl and Hjort (1976). Their calculation of the maximum annual growth rate under average conditions is 7.5%.

The figures also illustrate the growth rates over the years for the females, according to categories (calves, immatures and mature animals). In comparison, the incidence of young animals is higher in southern Somalia than in Case 2 of Dahl and Hjort.

In our southern Somalia case the female herd has doubled after 19 years and again after 34 years. The figures for Case 2 in Dahl and Hjort (1976) are not known: that herd does not double within 40 years. In their Case 1, the theoretical maximum growth case, the herd doubles after 11 years and again after 20 years. The proportion of female calves out of the total female herd after 40 years is in the Somali case 18%, in Case 2 of 13%.

The general conclusion for southern Somalia is that the situation there seems favourable. The camel herds surveyed exhibit a profile of youngish females, which indicates reliable growth and milk production for the future. We must point out the impact of the drought in 1976 and 1977, though since it caused a shortage in several age classes. A lack of reproductive animals is itself being reproduced. This case is discussed a bit further in the concluding section below.

MILK PRODUCTION IMPLICATIONS

The age of first calving is around four years (Mares 1954:418 for Somali camels and Williamson and Payne 1965:297 for the general case). This means, for our surveyed eleven herds, a composition of milking females, males and immatures according to Table V.

The age distributions in the herds vary considerably. We see that herd number 2 contains very many young animals, for instance, and herds 8 and 9 have few young ones. The proportion of mature males is nearly constant, slightly below 10%. The number of mature females represents slightly more than one third of the family herd in most cases. Again, herds 2 (with a small proportion of mature females) and 8 and 9 (with a high incidence of mature females) deviate while the aggregate has it that 35.69% are mature females.

For the sake of the discussion of milk production for family consumption, we shall assume that 36% of a herd in southern Somalia is made up of milking females and 16% of calves not yet weaned.

To begin with, this assumption does not distinguish between dry and milking herds in the samples. We have assumed that the herds surveyed have been a mixture, so that the aggregate represents an entire area herd. This is a fair assumption, given the area surveyed, one where both short-distance herding and long-distance trekking occurs. The long-distance herds might tend to be dry herds and the local herds milk herds.

Secondly, we will have to make an assumption concerning the proportion of lactating females. The survey was carried out in mid-1984 when conditions were not too detrimental. With fairly normal conditions and with the extended period of surveying in mind, we assume that half the number of mature females are lactating. The longish measurement period evens out the tendency for animals to reproduce during the Guu rains. Remaining is the herding strategy to have the female covered every other year. Thus we get a model family for the area according to Table VI.

The distribution in this empirical model coincides well with the model by Dahl and Hjort (1976:195) on the important points: proportion of calves and proportion of adult dams (17% and 34% respectively in Dahl and Hjort ibid). As a matter of fact the coincidence is so great that we may simply follow the work by Dahl and Hjort in calculating yearly yields from a model camel herd. This is done in Table VII.

We concentrate in this discussion on milk production. The assumption of 50% fertility has already been sufficiently discussed above in connection with the assumption of a 50% calving rate. An average lactation period of 12 months is typical for Somalia. An average daily yield of 4 kg of milk is also quite within what is reasonable for southern Somalia.

Dahl and Hjort (1976:104ff) have avoided the normal nutritional calculations based on the need of an individual and instead designed a reference family for pastoral circumstances. They have assumed a household made up of a father around 30 years, a pregnant mother of 25, two children of three and eight, and with one girl of 15 and one boy of 18 attached to the household. This reference family would require 318 g protein per day and 13 800 kcal.

With such a reference family the required family herd of camels, assuming that the family lives entirely on food produced from the family herd, has to have a size of 28 animals in total and with an age and sex distribution as in the model herd above.

CONCLUSIONS

One prime purpose of this study has been to present a practical method of estimating basic features of Somalia's camel population. It leads up to two major conclusions. One concerns the reproduction potential of the family herds in southern Somalia, and the other concerns their milk production potential. The sample in the present study is eleven herds but the approach could be replicated on a wide scale.

The reproduction potential for current family herds of camels in southern Somalia seems favourable. On the whole it falls within the interval given by Dahl and Hjort (1976) for camels, in fact, in the upper part. In comparison with herds in neighbouring northern Kenya, the Somali herds seem younger (Watson 1986). The projection (40 years on) shows a development full of vitality. Such projections of course do not account for droughts, which must be taken into concentration (see Dahl and Hjort 1979:10ff).

Food production in terms of milk output from the southern Somali family herds of camels seems to follow the results in Dahl and Hjort (1976:195) closely. We refer to their conclusions, inter alia, by suggesting at a required herd size of 28 camels to make a "typical" family self-sufficient in food, given that they live solely on milk. Of course, this is not normally the case. With a supplementary food intake of grain, adding energy intake to the surplus protein consumption, considerably fewer animals are needed.

REFERENCES

Dahl, G. and Hjort, A. 1976: *Having Herds. Pastoral Herd Growth and Household Economy*. Stockholm Studies in Social Anthropology, University of Stockholm.
Dahl, G. and Hjort A. 1979: "Pastoral Change and the Role of Drought", in: *SAREC Report*, R1, 1979.
Hjort, A. 1981: "A Critique of 'Ecological' Models for Pastoral Land Use", in: *Ethnos*, 1981:3-4:171-88.
Hjort, A. (ed) 1985: *Land Management and Survival*. Uppsala: Scandinavian Institute of African Studies.
Mares, R.G. 1954: "Animal Husbandry, Animal Industry and Animal Disease in the Somali Land Protectorate Ptl, Pt 2", in: *British Veterinary Journal*, 110:411-423; 470-481.
Watson, R. 1986: "A Programmetric Sampling of Camels to Deduce the Age Structure of their Populations in Southern Somalia", in: *Camel Forum*, Working paper No 12.
Wikberg, E. 1971: *Näringslära*. Stockholm.
Williamson and Payne, 1965: *Animal Husbandry*. London.

Table I. *Population structures of the surveyed eleven herds (% of population in age/sex category)*

	0-0.5		0.5-1		1-1.5		1.5-2		2-3		3-4		4-5		5-6		6-7		7-8		8-9		9-10		10	
	M	F	M	F	M	F	M	F	M	F	M	F	M	F	M	F	M	F	M	F	M	F	M	F	M	F
1	4.8		8.0		6.7		8.0		13.3		13.6		13.4		5.0		3.4		2.2		3.1		4.1		11.4	
	1.1	3.7	1.3	6.7	0.9	5.8	0.9	7.1	1.7	11.6	2.2	11.4	2.5	10.9	1.0	4.0	0.2	3.2	0.5	1.7	0.6	2.5	0.9	3.2	2.1	9.3
2	15.2		14.6		12.4		6.1		19.2		10.4		9.6		3.8		3.0		0.3		1.3		1.3		3.0	
	3.5	11.7	2.4	12.2	1.7	10.7	0.7	5.4	2.4	16.8	1.7	8.7	1.8	7.8	0.8	3.0	0.6	2.4	0.1	0.2	0.3	1.0	0.3	1.0	0.5	2.5
3	13.5		9.5		6.3		6.8		7.7		14.0		9.9		9.5		3.2		3.2		1.4		1.8		13.5	
	3.1	10.4	1.5	8.0	0.9	5.4	0.8	6.0	1.0	6.7	2.2	11.8	1.8	8.1	1.9	7.6	0.7	2.5	0.7	2.5	0.3	1.1	0.4	1.4	2.5	11.0
4	3.8		7.4		9.3		5.8		12.8		11.9		9.3		7.1		2.2		1.0		5.1		3.5		20.8	
	0.9	2.9	1.2	6.2	1.3	8.0	0.7	5.1	1.6	11.2	1.9	10.0	1.7	7.6	1.4	5.7	0.5	1.7	0.2	0.8	1.1	4.0	0.7	2.8	3.8	17.0
5	7.7		12.8		6.4		2.6		11.5		14.1		15.4		12.8		1.3		5.1		2.6		1.3		6.4	
	1.8	5.9	2.1	10.9	0.9	5.5	0.3	2.3	1.5	10.0	2.3	11.8	2.9	12.5	2.6	10.2	0.3	1.0	1.1	4.0	0.5	2.1	0.3	1.0	1.2	5.2
6	4.7		3.5		12.9		5.9		20.0		5.9		11.8		4.7		7.1		4.7		2.4		2.4		14.1	
	1.1	3.6	0.6	2.9	1.7	11.2	0.7	5.2	2.5	17.5	0.9	5.0	2.2	9.6	0.9	3.8	1.5	5.6	1.0	3.7	0.5	1.9	0.5	1.9	2.6	11.5
7	8.0		9.6		8.8		6.8		12.7		9.4		9.9		8.4		1.3		5.0		2.0		5.3		13.0	
	1.8	6.2	1.6	8.0	1.2	7.6	0.8	6.0	1.6	11.1	1.5	7.9	1.8	8.1	1.7	6.7	0.3	1.0	1.0	4.0	0.4	1.6	1.1	4.2	2.4	10.6
8	0		6.9		6.9		6.9		10.3		3.4		10.3		3.4		6.9		0		3.4		0		41.4	
	0	0	1.1	5.8	0.9	6.0	0.8	6.1	1.3	9.0	0.5	2.9	1.9	8.4	0.7	2.7	1.4	5.5	0	0	0.7	2.7	0	0	7.6	33.8
9	0		1.2		4.8		4.8		19.3		12.0		4.8		9.6		2.4		1.2		3.6		3.6		32.5	
	0	0	0.2	1.0	0.6	4.2	0.6	4.2	2.5	16.8	1.9	10.1	0.9	3.9	1.9	7.7	0.5	1.9	0.3	0.8	0.8	2.8	0.8	2.8	6.0	26.5
10	6.4		8.4		7.0		6.6		12.3		12.8		9.7		9.0		1.6		3.0		3.3		2.1		18.0	
	1.5	4.9	1.4	7.0	0.9	6.1	0.8	5.8	1.6	10.7	2.0	10.8	1.8	7.9	1.8	7.2	0.3	1.3	0.6	2.4	0.7	2.6	0.4	1.7	3.3	14.7
11	2.8		10.6		8.3		6.9		8.7		13.3		7.3		10.6		0.5		0.9		3.2		2.3		24.8	
	0.6	2.2	1.7	8.9	1.1	7.2	0.8	6.1	1.1	7.6	2.1	11.2	1.4	5.9	2.1	8.5	0.1	0.4	0.2	0.7	0.7	2.5	0.5	1.8	4.5	20.3
All	7.27		9.18		8.19		6.60		12.91		11.54		10.10		7.81		20.4		3.01		3.19		3.38		14.86	
	1.68	5.59	1.50	7.68	1.11	7.08	0.77	5.83	1.64	11.27	1.84	9.70	1.87	8.23	1.57	6.24	0.43	1.61	0.63	2.38	0.67	2.52	0.71	2.57	2.72	12.14

Source: Watson 1986

Table II. *The age distribution of female camels in eleven herds in southern Somalia*

	% of total herd	% of total female herd
0-1	12.5	15.2
1-2	12.5	15.2
2-3	12.0	14.5
3-4	8.5	10.3
4-5	8.0	9.7
5-6	6.0	7.3
6-7	2.5	3.0
7-8	2.0	2.4
8-9	1.5	1.8
9-10	1.5	1.8
10-11	1.5	1.8
11-12	1.5	1.8
12-13	1.5	1.8
13-14	1.5	1.8
14-15	1.5	1.8
15-16	1.5	1.8
16-17	1.5	1.8
17-18	1.5	1.8
18-19	1.5	1.8
19-20	1.0	1.2
20-21	1.0	1.2
	82.5	99.8

Table III. *Ratios female calves/mature females in the eleven surveyed herds*

Herd number	Proportion female calves 0-1	Proportion mature females	Ratio
1	10.4	34.8	0.30
2	23.9	17.9	1.34
3	18.4	34.2	0.54
4	9.1	39.6	0.23
5	16.8	36.0	0.47
6	6.5	38.0	0.17
7	14.2	36.2	0.39
8	5.8	53.1	0.11
9	1.0	46.4	0.02
10	11.9	37.8	0.31
11	11.1	40.1	0.28
All*	13.27	35.69	0.37

*The distribution of the aggregate established by the eleven herds

Table IV. *Assumed survival rates in % in the different age classes*

Age class	Dahl & Hjort, Case 2[1]	The aggregated surveyed herd	The model
0-1	70	?	70
1-2	78	97	90
2-3	86	87	90
3-4	94	86	85
4-5	98	85	85
5-6	98	76	80
6-7	98	26	80
7-8	98	148	98
8-9	98	106	98
9-10	98	?	98
10-11	98	?	98
11-12	98	?	98
12-13	98	?	98
13-14	98	?	98
14-15	93	?	93
15-16	89	?	89
16-17	84	?	84
17-18	79	?	79
18-19	75	?	75
19-20	70	?	70
20-21	58	0	0
21-22	47		
22-23	35		
23-24	23		
24-25	12		
25-26	0		

[1] Dahl and Hjort (1976:83)

Figure I. *The development of the model herd, Example 2 in Dahl and Hjort (1976:86)*

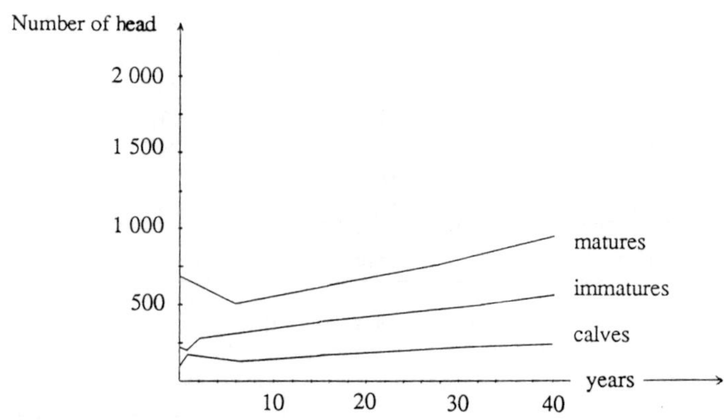

Figure II. *The development of the model herd for Southern Somalia over 40 years*

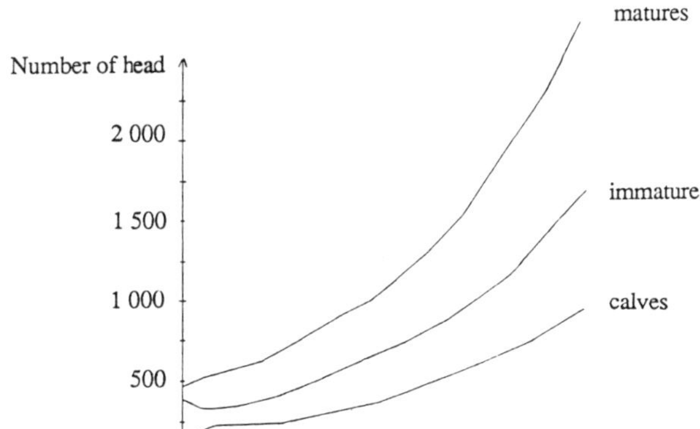

Table V. *The distribution of mature females, males and immatures in the eleven surveyed herds.*

	% of total				
Herd number	Calves 0-1 yr	Immatures	Mature males	Mature females	Total
1*	12.8	41.6	7.8	34.8	97.0
2	29.8	48.1	4.4	17.9	100.2
3	23.0	34.8	8.2	34.2	100.2
4	12.2	38.8	9.4	39.6	100.0
5	20.5	34.6	8.9	36.0	100.0
6	8.2	44.7	9.2	38.0	100.1
7	17.6	37.7	8.7	36.2	100.2
8	6.9	27.5	12.3	53.1	99.8
9	1.2	40.9	11.2	46.4	99.7
10	14.8	38.7	8.9	37.8	100.2
11	13.4	37.2	9.5	40.1	100.2
All**	16.45	39.24	8.60	35.69	99.98

* The proportional figures for this herd are inconsistent in that the total becomes less than 100%.
** The distribution of the aggregate established by the eleven herds.

Table VI. *The distribution of milking females, dry females, males and immatures in the model family herd.*

	Calves 0-1 yr	Immatures	Mature males	Milking females	Dry females	Total
Aggregate herd	16.45	39.24	6.60	35.69		99.98
Model herd	16	39	9	18	18	100

Table VII. *Yearly yields from the model camel herd of 100 animals.*

	Number of animals	Individual yield (kg)	Yield from all the herd (kg)	Protein (kg)	(kcal)
Milk	17	1,460	24,820	918.34	17,374,000
Meat	3	225	675	141.75	664,605
Hump fat	3	20	60	-	527,400
Total				1,060.09	18,566,005

Basic information used:

Milk: 50% fertility, 12 months lactation, average daily yield 4 kg milk with the following nutritive values: 4.2% fat, 3.7% protein, 4.1% lactose and caloric yield 700 kcal/kg.
Meat: 225 kg per carcass, containing 21% protein and 1% fat.
Hump fat: 20 kg per carcass

Transformation values kcal/g according to Atwater (Wikberg 1971, p 98): 8.79 for fat, 4.27 for proteins in meat.

Source: Dahl and Hjort 1976:197.

Map I. *Location of the sampled camel populations in southern Somalia*

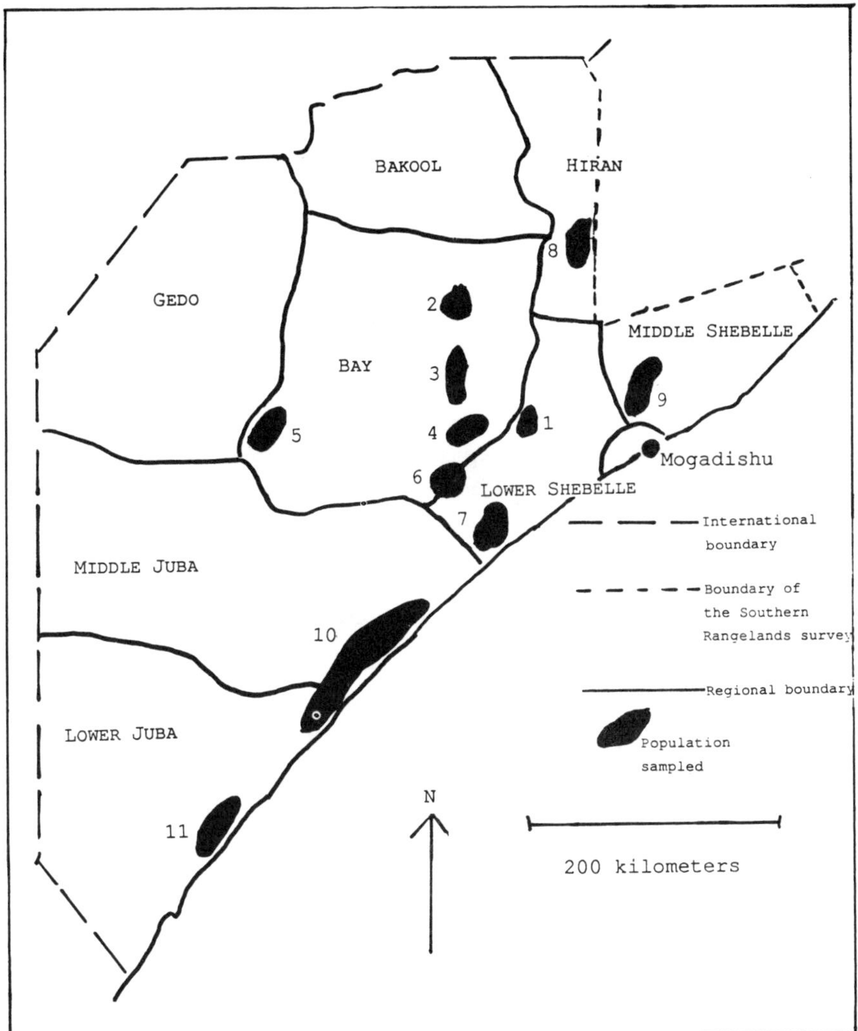

Source: Watson, M., 1986:9.

Discussant's Report

I. Eldisougi Mustafa

IGADD presentation

- The newly-inaugurated IGADD was welcomed as a regional institution in that part mostly concerned with camels.
- While difficulties, including political problems within one and the same member country are noted, they should not deter scholars from helping to promote camel husbandry.
- Some of the countries donating funds for camel welfare and research could help avoid unnecessary delay through direct agreements between their own and recipient research institutes (e.g. the Scandinavian Institute of African Studies with other relevant institutions in Africa).
- Establishment of a regional or, rather, an international camel research institute is a goal to coordinate research in Asia, Africa and South America.

African drylands and balanced camel production

- Research pertinent to camel husbandry is expected to receive further support, along with other areas.
- Meat, milk and milk products should be given due consideration. In addition, wool, hair and hides are marketable.
- Camels can also be used for transport, ploughing and cultivation.

Settlement Scheme for the Nomadic Pastoral Fulani of Nigeria: Some Relevant Issues

Moses O Awogbade[1] and Umaru A Hassan[2]

INTRODUCTION

There is no denying the urgent need to settle Nigeria's nomadic pastoral population, considering that the bulk of the country's livestock is in their hands: they own about 90% of the country's small and large ruminants and its small but not insignificant camel population.

In recent decades, traditional animal husbandry practices in the semi-arid lands has been gradually eroded by confiscation and appropriation of pasture lands by commercial ranchers and government agricultural policies, which favour crop production. As a result nomadic pastoralism has diminished and pasturage has contracted very rapidly.

Herding households have emigrated to neighbouring countries and the country's meat supplies have been severely depleted. 40% of slaughtered animals were from foreign sources between 1979 and 1983. These trends must necessarily have serious repercussions on the livestock industry, as well as on those whose livelihood is dependent on cattle rearing.

To increase livestock production, the government has intervened in various ways, which have included encouraging the nomads to settle, in the belief that settlement would increase productivity.

In this paper, we look at nomadic pastoralism as it affects livestock production generally and with a view to identifying factors that militate against the settlement scheme.

The first part discusses the issue of pastoralism and land use as it impinges on the husbandry system; the second part deals with settlement policy. The paper concludes by stressing what needs to be done to assist the government settlement scheme.

---

[1]Moses O Awogbade, Centre for Social and Economic Research, Ahmadu Bello University, Zaria.
[2]Umaru A Hassan, Department of Geography, Ahmadu Bello University, Zaria.

PART I

Pastoralism and Land use

Cattle rearing in Nigeria is still predominantly in the hands of Fulbe pastoralists, who constitute about 90% of livestock producers. The bulk (58%) of the meat supply and of livestock products come from their hands.

Their system of husbandry relies mainly on free range natural grazing and crop residues, which replace natural grazing during the larger part of the dry season.

The seasonal movements of nomadic Fulani in and out of their traditional grazing grounds are determined by the duration of wet and dry seasons, the extent of farmlands under cropping and access to markets where dairy products can be sold and consumer goods purchased. Movement in a predictable cycle has developed as the most effective method of exploiting the grazing resources (mainly water, natural fodder and crop residues) and taking advantage of veterinary services and market conditions (Awogbade, 1980).

Land use competition between animal husbandry and arable agriculture is often intense in the Sudan and Sahel Zones, which also carry some of the highest densities of human population in Nigeria. At best, cattle rearers and the sedentary agriculturalist have established a symbiotic relationship with mutual benefits: the pastoralists help in providing manure to the farmers fields in the dry season as they graze their animals on the crop residues. However, where access to crop residues is allowed, herders now commonly pay for the privilege of using them.

Through centuries, a set of rules has evolved for pasturing cattle on stubble and fallow land and for guaranteeing cattle tracks *(burtali)* and the use of water (Mortimore, 1978). Since crop damage by cattle has often led to litigation triggered by physical violence in which dangerous weapons have been used, farmers in most areas are beginning to see the pastoral Fulani as a serious threat to their livelihood.

There is also a basic problem with present animal husbandry practices and the rights of nomadic Fulani, who own most of the livestock. While grazing rights tend to be communal, farming rights are becoming increasingly individualized. Also, there has been a progressive extension of cultivation areas without concern for the preservation and development of grazing lands. In most cases, this has led to conflicts of interest between crop producers and pastoralists. While the courts could award damages for the destruction of crops by cattle, there seems to be no concern for the need to protect cattle routes from being converted into farms. This begs the important question of what access to land and pasture the pastoralists would have in future (Ega, 1984).

Contemporary land utilization in Nigeria obviously favours crop production and rapid and far-reaching changes are under way. For instance, uncultivated grazing lands, once the preserve of nomadic herders, have decreased from 67% in 1951 to 50% in 1976; and a further decrease of 39% is predicted for 1986 (Awogbade, 1981).

It is therefore quite clear that the relationship between the two users of land is bound to worsen in several areas of the country. There is already massive evidence to show that agricultural activities have reduced the "resource base" at the disposal of pastoral Fulbe, thereby accelerating conflict between users of rural land (Baba, 1986).

Rapid population growth, technological changes (including adoption of fertilizers and increasing use of tractors), as well as large-scale programmes such as those of Agricultural Development Projects (ADPS) and the River Basin Development Authorities (RBDAS) have all taken land from the pastoralists.

Mortimore (1986) notes that grazing rights are coming under increasing pressure. Open wood grazings are diminishing, with growing agricultural colonization, and pastoralists cannot usually dispute such appropriations. Riverine (Fadama) pasture is rapidly disappearing due to government construction of dams and irrigation channels. As grazing territories are being encroached upon, pressure mounts on the remaining open rangeland, productivity is diminished, established patterns of mobility are dislocated and court litigation is increased.

Competition between pastoral and agricultural producers for fertile land has brought about a persistent rift between them, especially in northern Nigeria, that could mean a set-back for the government settlement policy, especially in the absence of a well-formulated and well-administered land reform. This could result in a situation of pastoralists depending on the hospitality and goodwill of agricultural communities to gain access to the use of community resources.

The magnitude of land problems in rural areas of the country has been clearly demonstrated in Frantz's comments about the pattern of land use by pastoralists in Donga-Mantung and Mambilla communities in Cameroun and Nigeria respectively. Crucial problems concerning land use and land tenure remain to be worked out in Nigeria. Despite all efforts of government, livestock production is still inadequate to fulfil either the goals of government or demands of consumers. Obviously the land question is central to livestock development.

Although the Nigerian government seems to be aware of the bottle-neck posed by the land tenure system, which works against nomadic pastoralists, not much has been done to effectively tackle the problem. The recent land use act of 1978, which vested *all* land in the hands of the states, has hardly been enforced. As correctly indicated in Ezeomah (1985), the land use decree of 1978 established landholding ceilings: 500 hectares for agricultural purposes, or 5,000 hectares for grazing purposes.

But this law has hardly been enforced; nomadic pastoralists have not been able to seize the opportunity offered by the Act. Questions of land ownership and the exercise of user rights are still effectively controlled by local communities and individuals.

PART II

Government settlement policy

It would be wrong to assume that conflicting demands for land between arable farming and pastoralism have gone officially unrecognized. Available records show that right from colonial times concern had been raised about the shrinking rangeland and the attendant social and economic repercussions. In fact, reference has been made to this problem in various plan documents.

The thrust of official policy towards a solution, however, has been mainly in the direction of establishing "grazing reserves". Intervention such as this has one principal motivation - to raise production by settling the nomadic pastoralist. As early as 1949 grazing reserve had been identified in a World Bank report as a required strategy for guaranteeing pastoral nomads continued access to adequate rangeland.

It is assumed that within the established reserves, specific areas of land will be allocated to certain pastoral individuals and/or families and groups. Participants in such projects are usually required to give up age-old pastoral practices such as migrations and the right to decide on herd size and composition. In exchange the pastoralists will be provided with improved pasture, veterinary services, water, credit facilities, market services and literacy classes. It is on these lines that the former government of northern Nigeria drew up legislation, reserving areas permanently and solely for grazing activities. This legislation was eventually passed in 1965, but since then only small areas have actually been established (for details see Awogbade, 1984).

Government intervention in livestock rearing is quite explicitly stated in the different National Plans (1961:1970:1975: and 1981), which recognize that Nigerian resource endowments dictate that livestock rearing remains an adjunct of arable farming. The point of departure in these plans is the encouragement of nomadic herders to take to mixed farming, change their traditional production outlook and thereby improve their use of grazeable rangelands. The standard remedy is the establishment of grazing reserves, group ranches and the like and to help pastoralists to settle by providing infrastructure and land tenure rights.

About 20 million hectares of land are estimated to be required for this purpose. So far only 2 million hectares have been officially acquired (FLD, 1980).

Under the First Livestock Development Project (Phase 1), a start has been made in providing 10 ha plots to pastoralists who wish to settle, grow crops and establish fodder plots. Herd numbers are expected to increase by 20% and milk sales by 50%. The project areas are located in Kachia (Kaduna), Gujba (Borno), Udubo (Bauchi), Garkida and Sorau (Gongola).

It is unclear whether the policy of grazing reserves would in fact promote the settlement of nomadic herders, as anticipated. Certainly, grazing reserves, by providing the pastoralists with land security could play an important role as a catalyst in pastoral development, eventually allowing pastoralists to invest in forage production, as suggested by Nuru et al (1979). However, between statement of intent and belief in the appropriateness of the proposals there is still some distance.

Recent surveys in some of the established reserves have shown that little progress has been made. For instance, evidence from Udubo shows that inhabitants are typically sedentary pastoralists that have simply relocated from other areas. In Kachia, only 34 settled pastoralists have so far benefited since establishment of the reserve in 1970. The impression one gets from the Kachia experience is that it can only provide opportunities for a few of the pastoral communities.

The Camel Factor

From our foregoing discussion, it is clear that present efforts by the Nigerian government favour improvement in cattle, sheep and goat production; there is a strong development bias towards these animals. The camel has been entirely forgotten, an yet it is highly important in the semi-arid areas of Nigeria-Sokoto, Borno, Katsina and Kano states.

It would be wrong to suggest that the Fulani pastoralists do not keep camels as a source of wealth, or lack knowledge of camel husbandry practices (see Table 1). As pack animals or short distance transportation and as draught animals camels are basic to the pastoralists' economy. This is also true of small-scale farmers in northern Nigeria who keep a small number of camels as pack animals. To ignore this in development planning is to disregard the interest of the marginalized peasant population in Nigeria's semi-arid zones, where the majority of camels are found.

Some observable reasons why the camel occupies a position backstage in discussions of development issues are: (1) the Fulani who manage cattle and camel jointly are not known to attach the same socio-cultural and economic values to the camel, as compared to cattle and small ruminants. This is quite understandable if we consider that camels take longer to reproduce and reach peak performance compared with cattle; (2) camel husbandry is essentially localized in four states - Borno, Sokoto, Katsina and Kano - in semi-arid areas of Nigeria and practised by settled pastoral Fulani; (3) consumption of camel meat is limited to certain specific areas of Nigeria such as Borno, Kano, Sokoto and Katsina states, which have large concentrations of Muslims, while elsewhere, particularly in the South, camels are regarded as dirty animals; (4) camel's milk is consumed at household level and not sold to the public; and (5) camel rearing is small-scale compared to cattle rearing.

It is therefore not unexpected that camel production has been neglected in connecting with livestock development. We expect this trend to continue for some time.

However, it is interesting to note that outbreaks of rinderpest in 1983 somehow changed the back-stage position of the camel. With a loss of about 15% of the national herd to rinderpest, and a resultant meat shortage, more people started to appreciate camel meat, especially in camel-rearing areas, where a substantial number of these animals are slaughtered for meat.

Another important development is the government settlement policy, which continues to encourage settled pastoralists with camels to move into the reserves. Camel herding will surely contribute immensely to identifying ecologically-balanced land use practices.

A typical case is in Jakusko grazing reserve, an area of about 183,000 hectars located in the semi-arid area of Borno state. It is one of the World Bank-assisted projects for livestock development.

In a 1985 survey by the Nigerian Livestock Development Project, 96 out of 202 households were identified as keeping camels, 2-15 head per household (see Table). Another grazing reserve where camel production has been identified is Udubo, Bauchi state. The main attraction in these reserves is a constant supply of water throughout the year and an abundance of leaves.

The number of camels in Nigeria has yet to be ascertained. What is significant to our discussion is the fact that the movement of some settled and semi-settled pastoral Fulani into the reserves focussed the attention of Nigeria Livestock Project Department (NLPD) officials on camel pastoralism. In the first place, NLPD was forced to change its range use strategy, which must now take account of the carrying capacity of the reserve so as to include camels and their grazing habits. Secondly, management strategy (in terms of provision of feed and supplementary feed) has to be worked out individually for cattle and camel, which are traditionally herded together. It is believed that improvement in the provision of feed would improve the reproduction potential of camels which, in the long run, would encourage more Fulani to bring their camels into the reserve.

The prospect of improving camel production, especially in the semi-arid areas of Nigeria, lies not in subsistence oriented activities but as part of improving livestock production as a whole. This will be a long process, but the government has made a start.

The problems of grazing reserve

Notwithstanding the foregoing, it is still relevant to discuss whether grazing reserves can adequately fulfil the goals for which they have been established (i.e. settlement with a view to changing the inhabitants into agro-pastoralists).

Experience with Fulani pastoralists in Nigeria has shown that where settlement (usually spontaneous) has occurred, nomadic pastoralists are converted into agro-pastoralists. But their output of both livestock and crops is poor in both quality and quantity as they struggle for a livelihood with the resources (land, water, etc) available to them.

Now that the concept of grazing reserves has caught on in all the ten northern states, it is pertinent to discuss what we consider to be the crucial problems facing them.

The problems with the range reserves (as they are now constituted) raise doubts about their future prospects:

1. Since their establishment by the northern Nigeria government in the early 1960s, the reserves have attracted a large population of cattle, and the quality and quantity of herbage have declined as the grazing pressure increased. This in turn has meant migrations to areas outside the reserves for supplementary feeding.
2. Reserves are at best only a stop-gap measure (Baba, 1986). When successful (which they seldom are) they may enable some separation of crop land and pasture. The forces that created the need for reserves are primarily demographic, (i.e. the rising numbers of farmers and livestock) and cannot be abated by reserves. On the contrary, reserves can only encourage the rise of the cattle population and lead to further pressure on the available land, to land degradation, to migration and exacerbation of conflict with cultivators.
3. Grazing reserves have been developed as enclave economies in attempts to preserve the territorial and socio-cultural aspects of two distinct systems of production - pastoralism and arable farming.
4. Grazing reserves assume the existence of a favourable cultural milieu among nomads for purposes of facilitating settlement processes. Judging by the Nigerian experience, this is still contentious; and

5. A fundamental problem exists in terms of providing adequate grazeable land. With three to four hectares per head, 30 million hectares of grazing land is needed - that is, approximately one third of the country. Certainly the 3% of the population who practise animal husbandry could not be allocated 30% of Nigeria's land mass! The question is whether, in a country where landholdings are being fragmented, it will be possible to allocate large tracts of land for production of livestock. Obviously this is bound to create a new set of social and political problems.

Many of the grazing reserves that have been established to benefit pastoralists do not have very encouraging records. They rarely address the stated needs of pastoralists. In fact, it has been noted from research findings (Awogbade, 1984) that in spite of infrastructure having been made available, success in terms of the number of pastoralists settling voluntarily is very limited. Also there are few signs of improved production. These results can be attributed to several factors, including the following:

a. pastoralists have not been given the opportunity to obtain individual rights to land;
b. no serious attention has been given to ensuring that proposed reserves are ecologically suitable for livestock and acceptable to pastoralists;
c. pastoralists are hardly consulted regarding their perceived needs and wants, their wish for access to social services and their need to grow a limited area of crops;
d. those pastoralists who have so far settled in the reserves still lack easy access to improved methods of management and veterinary services;
e. areas set aside for graziers tend to be inadequate and with no effective policy on destocking, the usual result is over-grazing. Thus pastoralists are forced out of the reserves;
f. absence of socio-economic amenities such as markets, schools, health services which are necessary for a settled life;
g. some reserves harbour wild animals and have shrubs that hold the risk of uncontrollable bush fires;
h. the influx in the dry season of Fulani, who compete for the limited resources. (Also, their herds are always accused of spreading diseases.) Those who are already settled are forced out;
i. expenditure on the herds themselves is minimal, whereas greatest proportion of total expenditure is on staff and infrastructure.

PART III

What are the Prospects?

In the foregoing pages, we have looked at pastoralism and land use with a view to locate the problems that have militated against the settlement scheme and have indicated the problems facing the nomadic system of production. Central to these problems is the issue of land and the provision of adequate facilities for the migrating herds.

Thus far, the government has placed high priority on settlement and encouraged abandonment of the nomadic life-style in favour of sedentary livestock production. On the other hand, the environment in which animal husbandry is practised is usually not amenable. Conversely, when the environment is amenable, pastoralists have been known to become settled without policy interventions; and, as Awogbade (1985) notes, such a trend may well be a prelude to the evolution of the (seemingly elusive) stabilization of the settlement process.

Pastoralists are perhaps more immediately concerned with acquiring land titles than with changing their techniques of livestock production (Awogbade, 1985). This has been confirmed by recent studies in certain range reserves and by the position of Mietti Allah, a cultural organization which represents Fulani socio-cultural interests in Nigeria.

The government objective on the grazing reserve can be understood as twofold: to encourage gradual settlement of nomadic herders; and to create a base for the introduction of modern forms of agricultural management. Now that a start has been made in this direction in some range reserves, it is pertinent to ask: can the establishment of grazing reserves create an acceptable basis for the realization of this objective?

Data gathered from some of the reserves suggest that a security of land tenure is attractive to the nomadic pastoralists. Other attractions include the provision of dams and possibilities for producing forage.

Of equal importance is the question of how to direct further pastoral development in the existing range reserves. Going by what is actually happening is some reserves we visited, we offer the following suggestions:

1. In principle, settlement within the reserve should be regarded as a transitional stage, providing the means through which traditional cattle-owners can be encouraged to initiate modern forms of animal husbandry.
2. Experience has shown that grazing reserves are established anyhow and anywhere, without considering their suitability or otherwise. Ecological

studies should be the determining criterion for selecting an area as a grazing reserve.

3. Pasture development, through the cultivation of improved species of grasses and legumes that can carry productive animals throughout the year, should be rigorously pursued. Government extension workers should encourage pastoralists to manage pasture plots individually.

4. Reserves should be divided into paddocks for maximum utilization. In addition to pasture plots, pastoralists who agree to settle should be allocated about 3 ha of land for crop cultivation. Crop residues should be used as feeds during critical periods.

5. Construction of access roads and demarcation of cattle routes is highly necessary. In times of low rainfall or natural hazard, cattle routes could be used in a search for alternative grazing areas.

6. It is also necessary to provide adequate health services for both humans and animals; markets for cattle and dairy products; and schools for the education of Fulbe children.

7. Some grazing reserves have been deserted due to their lack of security and vulnerability to constant raids by bandits. Protection is needed against these raids.

8. The focus of grazing reserves should be on integrating the two groups of rural land users, caution should be taken to limit the extent of land cultivation.

9. Efforts to implement stock quotas should take into account, as a first priority, the number of people that are dependent on livestock for a living. In a situation where there are many people living off the quota, arrangements for them to make a living elsewhere must be made before enforcing the quota.

10. Any development scheme needs the support of the beneficiaries; pastoral development is no exception. Therefore, opinion leaders of pastoral Fulbe must be involved from the planning stage.

11. Public education programme on the need for mutual co-existence between nomads, farmers, law enforcement agencies and local leadership should be intensified; and

12. Surveys should be carried out in each grazing reserve, among pastoralists and non-pastoralists, to determine the viability of the settlement programme in terms of resource use and to obtain the views of those concerned. This calls for permanent engagement of rural development planners, sociologists and anthropologists. Besides conducting socio-economic surveys, this group of specialists will form time to time gauge the opinion of pastoralists and farmers so as to ensure that their "users' views" are reflected in the management of the reserves.

SELECTED REFERENCES

Awogbade, M.O. 1980: *Rural Development and Livestock Production: The Case for the Creation of Grazing Reserve.* Paper presented at the Centre for Social and Economic Research, Ahmadu Bello University, Zaria, Nigeria.

Awogbade, M.O. 1981: "Livestock Development and Range Use in Nigeria", in J. Galaty et al. (ed): *The Future of Pastoral Peoples.* Ottawa, Canada: IDRC.

Awogbade, M.O. 1985: *Nigeria Second Livestock Development Project: A Sociological Survey.* NLPD/FLD Publication.

Awogbade, M.O. 1986: "Grazing Reserves and the Pastoral Settlement Model in Nigeria." Paper presented at *The 22nd Annual Conference of the Agricultural Society of Nigeria,* Zaria.

Baba, J. 1986: "Reconciling Agricultural and Pastoral Land use Systems in Nigeria." Paper presented at *Land Resource Workshop,* Kano, Nigeria.

Ezeomah, C. 1985: "Land Tenure Constraints Associated with Some Recent Experiments to Bring Formal Education to Nomadic Fulani in Nigeria", in: *Pastoral Network,* O.D.I., England.

Galaty, J. and Salzman, P. 1981: *Change and Development in Nomadic and Pastoral Societies.* E J Brill, Leiden.

Gefu, J.O. 1986: "Land Utilization Pattern and Nomadic Pastoral Producers in northern Nigeria: The Sedentarization Issue Revisited." Paper presented at *Land Resource Workshop,* Kano, Nigeria.

Mai, M. 1986: "Settlement and Education of Nomadic "Fulbe"." Paper presented at *The National Workshop on Mobile Education for Nomads,* Yola, Nigeria.

Mortimore, M. n.d.: "The Lands of northern Nigeria: Some Urgent Issues." Paper presented at *Land Resources Workshop,* Kano, Nigeria.

Nuru et al. 1979: *Guidelines on the Development of Grazing Reserves A Memorandum for the National Council for Agriculture and Rural Development.* NAPRI, A.B.U., Zaria.

Okaiyeto, P. 1981: "Integrating the Cattle Production System of the Pastoral Fulani on the Tsetse Eradicated Belts of the River Basins Development Authorities." Paper presented at *The First National Conference on Tsetse and Trypanosomiasis Research in Nigeria,* Kaduna, Nigeria.

Ribadu, A.A. 1986: "Settlement and Education of Pastoral "Fulbe"." Paper presented at *The National Workshop on Mobile Education for Nomads,* Yola, Nigeria.

TABLE

Table 1. *Livestock Population - Jakusko Grazing Reserve, Borno State, Nigeria (1985)*

Cattle	Sheep	Goats	Camels	Horses	Donkeys
137,233	12,483	10,253	201	96	747

Owners	
Settled	116
Semi-settled	45
Nomadic	41
Total households with camels	96

Discussant's Report

Set Bornstein

There is and has been an urge to settle pastoral people. In the past scarce resources on the very marginal, arid and semi-arid lands in Africa and elsewhere were well utilized by pastoral people and their livestock were continuously on the move in search of food and water.

The nomadic way of life has always been a concern to national governments, who felt threatened by these often tough and rebellious people, who were difficult to control and to tax due to their unpredictable whereabouts.

Today, the existence of pastoralists is threatened all over the world. In many places in Africa they have been forced to over-exploit the soil due to the "hunger for land" by agriculturalists (individual farmers as well as agribusiness and parastatal organizations) and the devastating droughts in the 1970s and 1980s.

The land suitable for farming is the dry-season grazing areas for many of the pastoralists' herds. This competition for land usually favours the agriculturalists, who are better represented in the governments and more outspoken.

The point of settling people is not only to incorporate them into a market economy and a more "modern" social and economic life, but also to neutralize strife between the settled and the non-settled and to make the livestock industry more efficient.

As we have learnt the policy in Nigeria is to settle pastoral people, who own 90% of the livestock, including a small number of camels. There is a meat shortage in the country. Nonetheless, a large number of Nigerian pastoralists (Fulani) have "emigrated" to bordering countries with their herds to find adequate pastures.

The Nigerian government is very concerned to increase beef output so as to help make the country self-sufficient in food and thus save on hard-currency imports.

The authors - Awogbade and Hassan - stress the fact that land use and land tenure are different aspects of a very crucial problem that needs to be solved. Another fundamental problem posed by the authors is that the national herd, owned by 3% of the population, needs 30 million hectares of pasture - one-third of the land-mass of Nigeria!

Already during colonial times there was an awareness of the problem of diminishing rangeland. One solution was to establish grazing reserves, the explicit intention being to settle the pastoralists and thereby improve and increase livestock production.

Since then new grazing reserves have been established and the present government has adopted a similar policy. Nevertheless, overall the grazing reserves scheme failed. The authors point out several reasons, of a technical, social and organizational nature, for the failure.

For one thing, the scheme seldom satisfied the real needs of the pastoralists, whose voluntary participation in it was small. Also, it failed to increase production.

In the Jordanian case we found that the concerned people, the bedouins, who had been persuaded to settle by promises of modern houses, schools for their children, medical and social services, and good roads, sold their camels. After 2-3 years they found that the settlement schemes did not work. All their hopes and aspirations came to nothing and they found themselves destitute. By that time they had no camels left to help them return to their old way of life. Nor did they have money to purchase new animals.

These two examples of settlement schemes, although different in many ways, bring out the necessity for better planning for programmes covering many years, suitable areas for settlement projects. (Ecological suitability including carrying capacity of the range, scope for pasture improvement, availability of water, the possibility of growing crops for humans and livestock etc. are among the considerations. Socio-economic studies must be carried out as well to decide on the viability of a settlement programme in the chosen area. Also the necessity of engaging the pastoralists, of obtaining their views and participation, is of vital importance.

In areas where suitable land is scarce (e.g. Nigeria) introduction of unconventional animals might be interesting in trying to meet the otherwise impossible demands on available pasture land. Crop monoculture or with one type of livestock husbandry will eventually lead to a degradation of the range.

A mixed-livestock enterprise with conventional and unconventional animals might lead to a better and more profitable use of land. One example is to introduce ostrich farming, which has turned out to be quite profitable (e.g. in Southern Africa and Israel). There are several other unconventional animals that are also well worth considering!

Recommendations

During October 20-22 1987 an international group of scholars actively involved in camel research gathered at Furudal, Sweden, in order to discuss the drought problems in Africa and elsewhere. The purpose of the workshop was to compare experiences and look into the potential of camel rearing for food production, draught needs and income generation in arid and semi-arid lands. The meeting realized that the camel plays a significant role in specific parts of the world, not least those that are struck by drought and disaster today. It therefore recommended:

1) To document the proceedings of the workshop.
2) To form a committee to formulate a plan of action in order to follow up issues raised.
3) The meeting recognizes two general needs: A need for further information and for further research in the countries with significant camel population. A holistic perspective should be established taking into account the people's own conception of their problems and how to cope with them. These general needs can be itemized as follows:

A. Development of appropriate socio-economic policies to realize the potential of the camel.
B. More information on the status of camel production, marketing and research in countries with drylands.
C. Coordination of efforts to help destitute people in drylands where the camel is a valuable animal.
D. Effective use of existing regional and national institutions in countries with drylands in collaboration with parallel institutions in developing countries.
E. More efforts from donors, in collaboration with relevant regional and national institutes for development, of effective production, marketing and research. Research should be carried out in the socio-economic field, also in other fields such as genetic improvement, pasture development, disease and so on, as a basis for effective policies.

4) Adequate measures to fulfil the needs are many. The workshop draws some conclusions:

A. We welcome IGADD as one of the important regional institutions with a capacity to pull relevant national institutions together. Co-operation should also extend to other camel regions. Specific institutes on camel research are needed.

B. The interest of donors in camel rearing potential has to be attracted without delay.

C. Rather than relying on conventional cooperation between governments, donors should utilize their own research institutions as channels for aid.

D. Regional and South/South research cooperation should be encouraged to the largest possible extent.

E. The great regional differences have to be pointed out, since the way camels are used varies considerably.

F. Research topics for immediate study are many, for example:

- various production traits
- systems approach
- training and extension as an integrated whole
- holistic approaches that take account of the people's own conceptions of how to deal with the environment.

The issues under item 4 require further elaboration by the action group. We propose that this be done under the heading "Drought and effective dryland pastoralism".

Concluding Remarks:
Camels or people first?

Anders Hjort af Ornäs

In the project that is being discussed in this report we have emphasized a perspective, *Man with environment* and the need to operate the zone between research and implementation. We usually try to raise a word of warning against large-scale projects being established without ample knowledge about local conditions, both socially and environmentally. Such a warning is particularly relevant in the current situation, where one can see two alternative approaches; a technical/economic one seeking new autonomous production forms, and a people-first approach starting from below, dealing with the problems as they are expressed in nomadic communities. A typical example of the latter is a joint project between Stockholm University and SIAS, where camel herdsmen meet national scholars in camel producing areas in some African countries. That project is to be reported later.

The present project is directed towards engaging scholars from camel-raising countries and supporting interaction and other kinds of networking. We hope that it mobilizes an interest but also that it stimulates a debate over implementation of the findings from camel research. Basically: How should one try to combine the need for improved food production from current extensive herding practices with the introduction of new intensive methods? My worry is that the attraction of research into new methods are greater than those in improving current ones. This is why I have tended to formulate these concluding remarks a little bit as a word of warning: We need to put both camels and people first also within camel research.

The kind of knowledge I think is needed concerns existing production systems and their change. Camel production is today changing or has already changed structurally. We witness a concentration of ownership, a loss of manpower and accordingly less efficient management practices. We also witness a penetration by a monetary economy into a kinship-based resource distribution system. Traditional ways of circulating domestic animals according to kinship bonds (or friendship bonds) to those in need give way to individualized ownership and withdrawal from circulation of animals that have been upgraded or which have received veterinary treatment.

True, great contributions can be made by the veterinary side. Diseases can be cured and animals upgraded, so that production and yields can increase. True also, a shift to camel keeping will have positive ecological effects for many areas, either as a supplement to cattle-raising or as a one-hundred percent change. *But the fundamental question to me concerns not increased yield for the more wealthy of a rural population.* It concerns what shall happen to the poor people, so crudely defined by development aid organizations as "the target group". There is a basic distinction between sectorized, technical "solutions", and approaches that involve people.

I understand that Nordic aid should be devoted to the latter. And yet camel management, in itself male-oriented would easily turn into private enterprise, controlled predominantly by affluent men, especially if Western technology were involved. This would definitely move us away from democratic ideals in popular participation or other political goals, with Nordic development aid intending to mobilize the weaker strata of a population. It might, however, tie in with national development plans or with commercial undertakings.

Poor people (not least women, children and marginalized groups) are causing environmental imbalance in that they are obliged to make use of natural resources beyond what is ecologically sound. Generally speaking, however, they are victims of a mix of global, national and local circumstances that in the end lead to land degradation: Unfavourable North/South relations, regional political imbalances or a breakdown of local production systems, for instance, due to changes in control over assets. These victims must not be treated as causes of imbalances. We have to listen to their requirements, when it comes to camel management, not least in terms of water and pasture control. When we speak about putting people first in a development context we have to find viable solutions for <u>these</u> groups. This ambition means seeking to support existing or new local resource management systems, whether they are based on family, on neighbourhood or on some cooperative form. These are all topics that were very much present at the conference, as can be understood from the recommendations. However, they are also topics that need thorough research, and it seems very difficult to find much competence in these fields within the academic communities in many of the camel-raising countries.

The quickly emerging interest in camel production systems has a great potential but also poses a threat: if initiatives from the outside come before an understanding of camel pastoralism, unforeseen developments may occur. Great attention needs to be given to existing food production systems involving the camel in order to indicate their vulnerable points. Conclusions should be on two levels; how to support present systems, and how to create alternatives that do not risk destroying what already exists. An example: In extensive camel-rearing systems it might not be possible to upgrade the animals for increased milk production, but one might very well seek new techniques that are less labour intensive, ways of securing seasonal milk surplus through storable milk products, etc. In intensive camel rearing, milk production might be considerably increased.

One aim of the group that met in Furudal is to set up a research network on two levels; first, a widespread and comprehensive one, and then a close-knit one consisting of a few first-class research projects with fairly intense interaction in different countries. In focus is the camel *and* its context rather than merely the animal itself.

Cooperation should be built around production aspects and seek to fill gaps of knowledge about relations between animals and people, although it departs from a more general treatment of interrelations between the three factors of animals, land and people.

Much of the research work should be done within camel-raising countries. There is substance to the thought of a university under the tree: both applied and pure research are needed. The rather comprehensive work that has been done in Somalia over the last five years (see the Annex) falls into both categories. On the applied side it aims at eventually providing proposals for viable development projects. Currently we deal with seasonal camel milk dairies for town delivery, "traditional" veterinary medicines, disease control inputs, and making available knowledge and tradition inherent in a poetic oral tradition. The work aims at identifying bottle-necks, and finding appropriate measures to increase the factor of sustainability in people's established production systems, for instance by suggesting supplementary activities.

And I wish to emphasize that this is where development aid's mandate lies: to depart from problems as perceived by a local population. What is needed is not primarily an expatriate engagement in a suddenly fashionable camel racket. Rather than arranging internal Western meetings, we in the North should continue interactions with colleagues from the South who are in closer contact with the "victims" of development aid. People must come first. What we have to do is to better comprehend an often complex interplay between Man and his land and animal resources. We do not need very sophisticated Western knowledge from problem formulation, to model building, to evaluation, to recommendations. The great danger is that development aid contributes to a process of social stratification.

List of participants

Saeed Salman Abu Athera, Abu Dhabi, U.A.E.
Moses O. Awogbade, Centre for Social and Economic Development,
    Ahmadu Bello University, Zaria, Nigeria
Urgessa Biro, Scandinavian Institute of African Studies, Uppsala, Sweden
Set Bornstein, The National Veterinary Institute, Uppsala, Sweden
Ahmed El-Houri, Intergovernmental Authority on Drought and
    Development, Djibouti
Ayele Gebre Mariam, Addis Ababa, Ethiopia
Bo Göhl, Swedish Agency for Research Cooperation with Developing
Countries, (SAREC), Stockholm, Sweden
Anders Hjort af Ornäs, Scandinavian Institute of African Studies, Uppsala,
    Sweden
N.D. Khanna, National Research Centre on Camel, Bikaner, Rajasthan,
India
Christer Krokfors, Scandinavian Institute of African Studies, Uppsala,
    Sweden
Carl Fredrik Liungman, Ministry for Foreign Affairs, Dept for International
    Development Co-operation, Stockholm, Sweden
Henrik Secher Marcussen, International Development Studies, Roskilde
    University Center, Roskilde, Denmark
I. Eldisougi Mustafa, Agricultural Research Council, Khartoum, Sudan
Mohamed Abdillahi Rirash, La Nation, Djibouti
Mohamed Ali Hussein, Somali Academy of Sciences and Arts, (SOMAC),
    Mogadishu, Somalia
Mohamed A Mohamed Salih, Scandinavian Institute of African Studies,
    Uppsala, Sweden
N. Shanmugaratnam, Norwegian Centre for International Agricultural
    Development, (NORAGRIC), Ås-NLH, Norway
Frode Storås, Center for Development Studies, University of Bergen,
    Bergen, Norway
Julio Sumar, IVITA/Universidad Nacional Mayor de San Marcos, Cusco,
    Peru

Secretariat

Susanne Linderos and Anne-Marie Vintersved, Scandinavian Institute of
    African Studies

Somali Camel Research Project: Project Presentation, September 1987

Anders Hjort af Ornäs
Mohamed Ali Hussein and
Christer Krokfors (eds)

OBJECTIVES AND CONTEXT

The Somali camel research project began in 1982 as a joint Somali/Swedish undertaking. It is financed by SOMAC (the Somali Academy of Sciences and Arts), and SAREC (the Swedish Agency for Research Cooperation with Developing Countries). It is coordinated from SOMAC by Mohamed Ali Hussein and from the Scandinavian Institute of African Studies (SIAS) by Anders Hjort af Ornäs .

The project aims at understanding the role that the camel has to play in Somalia. Planners must be supplied with detailed knowledge so that new development projects do not create imbalances in the ecological interplay between humans, camels and pastures. Among other things, one must also realize the cultural importance of the camel; this is the concern of one sub-project. A number of subprojects are concerned with how life as a camel herdsman could be improved; seeking modified forms of camel husbandry which are less labour intensive. Much can be done about camel diseases. Milk production can be increased and new dairy products need to be developed. Local trade to small towns and centres could be improved. The knowledge of camel herdsmen needs to be fed into the planning process. Attention must be given to boundary areas where camel herding competes with farming or other land use practices.

The interest in the camel has grown lately, following the upheavals of drought disasters. It seems that camel herding offers *one* important contribution towards finding sustainable solutions in the long run. Camel husbandry is by-and-large the only realistic means of food production without causing soil erosion in huge tracts of fragile lands. Milk production of the camel is excellent, considering the environmental circumstances.

The camel in Somalia is to a large extent kept as a milk animal although camel meat also figures in the diet. Camel hides give an extremely strong leather. As a transport animal, the camel is excellent for short distances, i.e. those local movements of goods which never appear in official statistics.

Livestock form the backbone of the Somali economy. Of its citizens, 80 % are engaged in one form of animal husbandry or another, and 70-90 %

of the country's export revenues derive from the livestock sector. The main destination of exports is Saudi Arabia, in the past Somalia has supplied more than half of that country's imports of meat.

The livestock population of Somalia is made up of camels, cattle, donkeys, sheep and goats. There are between five and six million camels, mainly in the northern and central parts of the country. Counting camels is, however, extremely difficult. Seasonal migrations, movements across national boundaries, and reluctance of the local population to give herd sizes, among reasons. The censuses are accordingly not quite reliable.

Camel exports account for approximately one tenth of total revenues from livestock exports or some 8 % of total Somali export earnings. Government expenditures in the livestock sector (some 15% of the budget) seem weak considering its dominating role. Interest in the camel is particularly meagre. These facts provide strong incentives to carry out research on the camel that can provide reliable information on which to base future planning, and investments.

The greatest importance of the camel is that it enables most Somalis to produce their own food in a subsistence economy. They do so under extremely varying conditions including, once every 6-8 years, during droughts.

In Somalia one can identify a number of food production systems in which camel husbandry is of importance. One is agro-pastoralism, a combination of farming and animal husbandry. Another is pastoralism combining different species of livestock and/or a diversification of family herds into several management units. Whatever the food production system, one also has to consider how it is linked with the urban monetary system.

In the case of pastoral household, a balance needs to be struck between (i) the number of humans available in the pastoral enterprise, (ii) the number of domestic animals, and (iii) availability of forage, water and salt. Each of these components is directly or indirectly dependent on the others. The herd size, for example, is not a function only of biological growth. It is also constrained by management decisions, herding practices, available manpower, forage and access to salt. Man's ability to make ends meet of course relates to food production from the domestic herd, also to labour needs for efficient herding and husbandry. A balance has to be struck between these consumption and production aspects if the household's viability is to be maintained.

This simple kind of ecological model for a balanced food production system is not sufficient to summarize today's conditions, since other factors complicate the picture or interrupt the balance, even at a household level. Given a risky life situation, individual households can diversify their productive activities, e.g. by rearing other animals or going into farming. The penetration of a capitalist economy into that of camel pastoralism implies changes, including changes in the distribution of wealth. The trend is for camel ownership to be concentrated in the wealthy strata of the population, while there is a reduction in herd size for the majority along with an increased economic diversification. Another factor may be limited access to pasture, due to a growth of competing land use practices, for example, over dry season pastures. Labour migration out of a pastoral system is yet another factor. One acute inherent conflict is that between the need for able-bodied men for the management of camel herds in Somalia, and the pull from the labour markets, especially those in the Middle East.

The issues mentioned here on a general level quickly lead to questions of an interdisciplinary nature. The intention is to hint at a complexity which needs to be recognized.

A number of development projects, especially in the field of range development, may have effects on camel husbandry. It is not obvious that all are beneficial to the camel, or even to those production systems of which camel husbandry forms a part. An increasingly important result of the work of the Somali project scholars is the contribution to development projects in the country.

Obviously one of the tasks of research on camel husbandry in Somalia is to make projections of alternative developments. Such projections include (i) extrapolations from the current situation that take into account of constraints such as those listed above, (ii) identification of activities that could complement present production systems, and (iii) study of alternative camel rearing practices.

The Somali Camel Research Project has successfully managed to mobilize research interest in Somalia. There was practically no camel research in 1981, whereas today an increasing number of Somali researchers are engaged in the project, looking at various aspects, from the perspectives of humanistic and social sciences to those of the natural sciences and technology. The approach in the project is interdisciplinary in the sense that one tries to integrate the various perspectives. In reality this is achieved through striving to illustrate each problem from several scientific points of view, keeping the interest of a local population in mind.

PROJECT PHILOSOPHY

One foundation stone of the project is that work is carried out primarily by Somali researchers. Only four Swedish researchers are at present engaged occasionally in the project, mainly as advisers and referees. The idea behind this is that research should be thoroughly anchored in the Somali research community so as to avoid a neo-colonial situation where expatriate researchers benefit most.

The formulation of subprojects thus depends on the availability of Somali researchers rather than on immediate research requirements. This approach has to be judged against the alternative of short-term, intensive expatriate inputs, which often lead only to technical solutions of development problems. The camel project aims at seeking a more profound understanding of the role of the camel today and its potential for improving conditions in the future. To reach such improvements, especially for the poorer strata of the rural population, it is important to use already existing knowledge about the camel and its relation to the physical and social environments. It should be recognized that the Somali people are going through a period of transformation from a society of oral communication to one where written language is increasingly used. The Somali researchers, deep insights into Somali culture and language is a prerequisite: they must transform orally- expressed knowledge into relevant research projects, and disseminate the outcome back to local planners, administrators and camel herders.

This philosophy of the project leads to an emphasis on long-term (at least a decade), low-profile, and localized research activities with a superimposed interdisciplinary approach. The possibilities to undertake such research are improved thanks to the field station at Yaq Bariweyne, which will also function as a base for on-pasture research on camel herds.

To immediately disseminate research results back to the camel herding society also implies new ways of reporting than those commonly used in scientific projects. Seminars where researchers and camel herders come together for discussions about current problems have already been successfully arranged.

The writings of scientific reports and articles is being improved through special courses. Wherever possible, the project will be regionalized and cooperation sought with researchers in neighbouring countries.

The interdisciplinarity of the project is manifested in a number of ways. The scholars carry out field work in groups of normally 3 - 4 persons, an approach that is appreciated both by scholars and local communities. In addition the scholars have regular meetings at Yaq Bariweyne the last weekend every month.

PROJECT STRUCTURE

The range of issues that need to be researched is great. When the project was initiated, a list of forty immediate research topics were identified through discussions between Somali camel herdsmen and the researchers. To encourage such research work, provided there are Somali scholars, available might easily lead to a fragmentation of activities - a matter which has been discussed internally in the project.

The interplay between the camel herd and the family managing the herd is emphasized. The project seeks to strike a balance between humanistic and social sciences, on the one hand, and natural and veterinary sciences, on the other. Some of the on-going subprojects are specialized within either of the two perspectives but they all have to refer back to the major project theme: to seek improved sustainability in rural Somalia. The interplay between issues of importance to the herd and the family gives rise to questions which lie at the roots of the project.

The current concentration is on three themes, with one researcher responsible for each (as well as for a subproject):

1. *The herd:* Topics concern the health status and disease of camel herds, camel forage, trypanosomiasis, reproduction, traditional veterinary medicine and zoonotic diseases.
2. *The family:* Camel management and migration, camel oral tradition, camel marketing, camels for men and women, and early domestication of camels.
3. *The herd and the family:* Camel milk proteins and cheese production, camel milk production and composition, herd dynamics, breeds and conceptual classification and, in a more specific way, the herd and the family. Research concerning the possibilities of a camel dairy plant is also carried out.

RESEARCH COMPLETED 1982 - 1986

The different subprojects are presented below. The researchers and institutions involved are also mentioned while publications from the subprojects are listed separately.

Camel management and labour migration
Mohamed Ali Hussein, SOMAC

The first part of this subproject has been carried out under the heading "Traditional camel husbandry". The purpose is to get access to, and analyse herdsmen's knowledge of camel husbandry in order to better understand the kinds of decisions that have to be made in different situations. Such information is urgently needed in order to comprehend pastoralists' reaction to various development projects in their areas. Field work was initially done in the central and southern parts of Somalia and later on extended to Mudug and Nugal. It was not possible to go to the important camel herding areas far north. However, some information has been collected from civil servants in these areas about an acute labour shortage.

Information has been acquired about camel management and labour problems as well as on household and herd composition through intensive field work in Gedo and Bakool regions and in Middle Juba and Lower Shebelle. The main topics of investigation are: How many people are required to take care of fifty camels? What is the cause of labour shortage (town migration, migration to Arab countries, or a shift to agricultural activities)? Altogether 55 families were interviewed.

Camel milk proteins

Muctar Ali Mohamed, Somali National University, and Märtha Larsson-Raznikiewicz, Swedish University of Agricultural Sciences

The objectives of this subproject are to provide new information on the chemical, mainly protein, properties of camel milk. The practical issue behind the subproject is how to make camel milk and milk products available to a wider range of consumers, especially as there is substantial seasonal over-production. Cheese making is one of the aspects. Attempts to make cheese from camel milk have been difficult. The composition and properties of the casein (cheese protein) as well as the mineral composition are important factors affecting the technical behaviour of the milk. The composition of the milk itself is known to vary with (for example) the age of the camel, number of calvings, lactation period, and the feeding conditions. Also, the water supply is of utmost importance.

Milk samples have been obtained from various kinds of herds in the area between Wanla Weyn and Bur Hakaba, about 150 km from Mogadishu. Milk from the 12 different camels thus sampled were analysed for pH, density, ash, fat, total nitrogen, and non-protein nitrogen. The total protein, total solids and not-fat total solids were determined.

After the identification of the main chemical properties of camel milk, the interest has been mainly concentrated on the caseins. Four casein components have been isolated. Amino acid and phosphorous analyses revealed that proteins analogous to the α_{s1}, -α_{s2}, -β and κ-caseins of cow milk occur in camel milk. Camel κ-casein shows some peculiar properties. It was, for example, impossible to identify this casein at all in most of the samples studied. The κ-casein plays several special roles in milk. For example, it gives milk its colloidal stability, and the enzymatic digestion of a single peptide bond in κ-casein causes all caseins to form a coagulum, the primary step in cheese formation. In order to better understand some of the technical problems associated with camel milk and to improve production of camel milk products, methods must be devised for purifying camel κ-casein so that the properties of this casein can be thoroughly studied. The difficulties in making cheese of camel milk is seen to be associated with shortage of κ-casein or with some properties of this casein.

Camel milk composition
Ahmed Mohamed Hashi, SNU

Through representative sampling in various parts of Somalia knowledge is gained about the chemical composition of camel milk. This is needed in various other subprojects for calculating nutritive qualities of food intake among camel herders. The work within this subproject has been undertaken in close cooperation with the work on camel health status.

Camel oral literature
Ahmed Ali Abokor, SOMAC

Camels are loved more than any other domestic animal by the Somali herdsmen because of their economic and social value. The special position of the camel is frequently expressed in Somali poems, metaphors, proverbs and tales of wisdom, of which there is a vast quantity. This literature is oral and has through generations been passed from father to son. The aim has been to collect and analyse this oral material. Ahmed Ali Abokor has presented the collection in a book in Somali language and an English translation has been made more recently by Ahmed Arten Hange.

Camel health and disease

Several veterinary subprojects have been included under this heading:

Camel disease survey
Fatuma Mohamed Jama, Serum and Vaccine Institute, SVI

Post-mortem examinations of more than 180 camels have been conducted - a joint effort between the project and the National Veterinary Institute in Uppsala, where the researcher was trained under Hans-Jörgen Hansen. However, the analyses were not concluded during this period.

Some features of the disease panorama of camels in Somalia
Set Bornstein, National Veterinary Institute, and Fatuma Mohamed Jama, SVI

Of the 184 serum samples from the camels post-mortemed by Fatuma Mohamed Jama, 125 have been tested for the three viruses IBR, P13, and BVD and for the protozoa toxoplasma. Tests to find antibodies against

Brucella abortus were also made on these sera. A further 40 sera from slaughtered camels in Mogadishu, 17 from Kisimayo, and 20 from different unspecified parts of Somalia were also screened. Some interesting results were obtained. Antibodies against parainfluenza-3-virus were quite common. Over 40 % of the 125 sera from camels slaughtered at Afgooye have titres above 1/16, and about 30 % showed a titre of 1/8. All the camel sera from Afgooye and from Kisimayo were negative regarding the IBR (infectious bovine-rhino-tracheitis virus). The 20 sera from different parts of Somalia showed over 50 % positive titres to IBR. Antibodies against bovine diarrhoea virus have been detected in a few camel sera from Afgooye and in over 50 % in the sera from different parts of the country. Regarding the screening for toxoplasma antibodies, the Sabine Feldman dyetest was made as being the most reliable test, applicable to all animal species. However, the CIA test seemed not to work on camel sera.

The health status of Somali camel herds
Hersi Guleed, SNU

As far as mastitis is concerned, the field data collected have shown that infections of the udder are significantly present in the camel populations of Lower Shebelle and Bay regions. Tick injures, milking practices, management methods and not least hygiene seem to play an important role in exposing milk glands to pathogens. Further infections might be brought about by ineffective hygiene, viz. unclean milkers' hands, methods used to milk camels etc.

Acute and chronic cases of mastitis were observed during the survey. The infected quarters have in some instances recovered spontaneously, in other cases become chronic. In addition to markedly reduced milk yields, stock owners have also referred to losses in camels and concomitant starvation of calves. However, reliable knowledge of the micro-organisms causing the disease of the udder in camels has not been obtained. Hersi Guleed continues his herd surveys and makes detailed accounting of camel diseases and injuries in selected camel herds.

Hersi also studies *shimbir* together with Set Bornstein. He has made investigations on the efficacy of Vernonia Mogadoxensis in goats infested with Sarcoptic Scabiei, and has been able to show that the use of Vernonia against mange on goats had very positive effects. Also, with Set Bornstein, he has initiated studies of the effects of Vernonia on camel mange.

In cooperation with another SOMAC/SAREC project, the camel project has studied traditional veterinary medicine; initially, the production of medicine in Somalia against mange.

Camel trypanosomiasis
Mohamed Farah Diriye, Ministry of Livestock, Forestry and Range

Mohamed Farah Diriye has undertaken his studies on camel trypano-somiasis in connection with his work with the tsetse fly eradication pro-gramme. It was shown that trypanosomiasis in camels of Somalia is quite prevalent. Although the number of animals tested was rather restricted, the findings were similar to those in other countries with large populations of camels, out of 336 tested 41 were trypanosome infected and 39 of these harboured Trypanosoma evansi. The known vectors of T. evansi are different tabanid (*Tabanidae*) flies. The other two positive cases were found to be Trypanosoma brucei and Trypanosoma congolense, two trypanosomes primarily infecting cattle. The vectors of the latter trypanosomes are tsetse flies. A safe conclusion is that Trypanosoma evansi is the main cause of camel trypanosomiasis.

Camel herd dynamics
Mohamed Ali Hussein, SOMAC, Anders Hjort af Ornäs, SIAS, and Christer Krokfors, SIAS

One limiting factor to economic expansion is the slow biological reproduction capacity of the camel. Information on age and sex structures of family herds is crucial both in order to comprehend current output and to extrapolate the herd's productive behaviour in the future. An understanding of herd dynamics (that is, biological reproduction, spatial distribution and social redistribution) is one way of approaching the question of how ecology, social organization and cultural systems relate. Such systemic knowledge is necessary for proper insight into the conditions of pastoral production systems.

Herd dynamics are important also for a variety of other specific reasons: (i) fluctuations and imbalances determine many management decisions, (ii) they relate to variations in milk production, (iii) they have decisive impact on herd reproduction, and (iv) they indicate the vulnerability of a herd to drought or other disaster.

The intention of this subproject has been to elaborate a method whereby age and sex compositions can be estimated through combined aerial and ground surveying. The method has been tried on a eleven nomadic herds. As a by-product, the map material used for the aerial surveying could be used for a study of seasonal migrations.

Camel browsing and grazing
Ahmed Abdi Elmi, SNU

Activities in this project began in March 1983. The focus of the research has been:

a. Distribution of camels in the different regions. Such information is of course needed for the selection of the proper sites for the research on browsing/grazing behaviour, rumination behaviour, water intake and collection of plant species for further chemical analysis.
b. Browsing (grazing) behaviour. The study has included: (i) ways of grazing: time of grazing, distances covered, rest time, and idle time. (ii) grazing cycle of the day (dawn, noon, dusk etc), (iii) amount grazed, (iv) factors affecting grazing; temperature, season, availability of palat-able species, preferences, age, and (v) effects of browsing on plant species.
c. Rumination, including observations on rumination time, and relations between rumination and browsing.
d. Drinking. This study includes observations of drinking behaviour, time of drinking (by seasons), water intake as influenced by breed, age of animal, dry matter intake, temperature, salty contents, pregnancy etc, and the relations between water and food intakes.
e. Chemical analyses of palatable plants. Attention is given to soil, season, stage of growth, physical characteristics of the land and plants.

A great number of plants have been collected and their Somali and Latin names recorded. A substantial number of plant parts (leaves, young shoots) and whole plants have also been collected and dried for later chemical analysis.

Camel breeds and classification
Mohamed Ali Hussein, SOMAC

The aims of this pilot project have been to commence examination of the variations in breeds or types in order to establish a basis for further decisions concerning improvement for meat and/or milk production. It is important to investigate to what extent the camels in Somalia are biologically different and to what extent variations are caused by varying ecological conditions.

Almost all parts of central and southern Somalia have been visited and information gathered on the different types of camels. The method has been to make observations of hundreds of animals in order to identify differences relating to: (i) size and weight, (ii) colour, (iii) milk production:

daily milk yield, lactation yield etc, (iv) maturity age, (v) distribution and habitat, and (vi) resistance to adverse environmental conditions and disease.

As well as data collection and observations in the field, some literature reviews have been made on material available on camel breeds and types in Somalia. Unfortunately, most of the earlier classifications are either according to locality or based on names of clans that tend particular types of camels.

Camel marketing and commercialization
Mohamed Said Samantar, SNU

The intention of this subproject has been to study the marketing of camels and camel products and the overall tendencies to commercialize the subsistence economy of the camel pastoralists. Internal sales of camels at certain market places in and around Mogadishu, Wanleweyn and Qoryoley have been studied. The main focus has been on: (i) numbers of camels sold at the market and those slaughtered, (ii) price variations during different seasons, and (iii) the collecting process and marketing of camel products (predominantly milk) and seasonal price variations.

After these investigations two topics have been studied. The first concerning the network of middlemen, followed the chain of deliveries from the producer to the consumer. The price changes have been mapped along with the network relations between middlemen. The second concerns exports and has included investigations of data on Somali camel exports and Saudi Arabian imports. The price fluctuations were also recorded.

A number of university students have been engaged in this subproject to carry out different studies on the camel economy. During 1986 three theses were completed: (i) Akrim Mohamed Farah: *The future of nomadic pastoralism* ; (ii) Ahmed Hussein Dirie: *For better utilization of camel meat;* and (iii) Ali Noor Farah: *The future of camel as a dairy animal.* Mohamed Said Samantar encouraged the students to write in English. The methods have been considered a bit unusual at the economic faculty in that they involve collecting primary data, something that students do not usually do. The students experienced practical methodological problems, but afterwards admitted that their training had been much better than a literature study.

CURRENT RESEARCH ACTIVITIES (1987 AND 1988)

The emphasis in on-going research is on the interplay between the camel herd and the family managing this herd - a fundamental theme also during earlier research. The different subprojects are all logical expansions of earlier research themes.

The Herd

During 1987 a field station was established at Yaq Bariweyne and a mobile laboratory is based there (see below). Most subproject activities are connected to the field station and the laboratory. Hersi Guleed is the sector coordinator for subprojects with the assistance of the Dean of the Veterinary Faculty, Abdulhamid Haji. Set Bornstein is adviser and consultant.

Health status and disease of camel herds
Hersi Guleed, SNU

This subproject is a continuation of the projects already started during earlier research periods. The purpose is to gain information about the typical ("average") camel herd, its health and disease situation, population structure and the dynamics of growth through the years.

The researcher returned to Somalia from veterinary training in Sweden in the latter part of 1986. During 1987 he continued investigations of health status. This study is divided into a general survey and a mastitis survey.

General survey
Field work concentrates on a number of selected herds, some of which have already been studied during previous phases of the subproject. The field work is undertaken mainly in Lower Shebelle and Bay regions. Much emphasis is placed on establishing close and trusting contacts with camel herding households and camel herders. The point of entry is to provide veterinary advice and to explain the purpose of the study. To establish close contact is sometimes a time-consuming process. The same is true of locating selected herds in the pastures during different seasons of the year. Therefore, the number of herds and animals that are included in the investigations are limited. The study is structured as follows:

(i) *The owner and his herd(s)*. The following background information is collected:
- name(s) of camel herd owner(s), place of living, family conditions etc.
- number of animals in the herd, their sexes, ages, dry or lactating females, pregnant females, serving mates etc.

- the name of the place where the herd is located at the time of investigation.
- the movements of the herd since the previous season (wet/dry/ intermediate).
- information on the environmental conditions in the present place, including existence of wild life, the quality of the pasture and water, plants that are considered by the herders as poisonous, humidity, temperature etc.
- the disease histories of the herd as told by the attendants of the camels, and the present health status of the animals.

(ii) *The health status of herds*. The ambition is to investigate all individual animals in the herd clinically to assess the health status of the herd. The general examination accounts for: sex, age, general appearance, pregnancy, stage of lactation and milk production (litres/day), body temperature, and skin inspection. The following are also systematically examined; mucous membranes, palpable lymph glands, the heart, lungs, rumen by palpation, percussion, and osculations.

(iii) *Laboratory tests*. Blood is checked for parasites and for general blood parameters. Faeces are tested for occurrence of parasites (eggs and larvae). Ecto-parasites are identified. Also, some chemical analyses of blood and urine are made.

Sensitivity tests of different strains of bacteria found in mastitis milk are performed and an evaluation of the most therapeutically efficient antibiotics is undertaken.

This subproject relates to several other projects, both on the "herd" side and the "family" side. As far as the former are concerned there is cooperation with the Swedish Agricultural University, for advanced technical assistance, and with the Serum and Vaccine Institute for identification of bacterial colonies. In the case of the latter there is cooperation with the "herd dynamics" project. Close cooperation is also maintained with the "milk production and composition" subproject.

Mastitis survey
The diseases of the udder of the camel are of major importance to the herding communities since milk constitutes a vital part of the food intake.

The impact of mastitis on milk yield is still to be assessed along with the wider prevalence in the country. In fact, the disease is not only present in camels but also in cattle and goats. The purpose of this work, carried out through field work and laboratory tests, is to collect basic data on the pathology of mastitis and its effect on milk yield and milk composition. Up to now, research on camel mastitis has been very limited and only a handful of references can be found in the literature.

In the course of field investigations herds are contacted several times, either on the pastures or at camps. Females are clinically investigated for mastitis and other infections. The status of the udder and the animal are described; a detailed life history of the females with signs of mastitis is recorded; a history of mastitis in the herd (epidemological) is noted; samples of milk and secretations from the udders of healthy and diseased camels are collected, and investigated for cell content and bacteria.

Camel range
Ahmed Abdi Elmi, SNU

This subproject is a continuation of "Camel browsing and grazing", initiated in 1983 . Before modern principles of livestock production can be applied to camels, detailed information is needed on their feeding behaviour in different ecosystems, about which little is known. Such information is also important for an understanding of the camels' survival mechanisms in both wet and dry seasons and during droughts. The study concentrates on free-ranging but herded camels in Leego area in Lower Shebelle region. This area is suitable for several reasons: (i) camel research has been going on in the area since 1983 and it is easy to sample Somali camel pastoralists; (ii) the nomads of this area are aware of on-going camel research and co-operation is easily established; (iii) the project's camels are taken care of by camel herders in the area; and (iv) Leego is at a relatively short distance from Mogadishu and for logistic reasons suitable as a research area.

The specific objectives include the following aspects on foraging behaviour of free-ranging camels: (i) time spent foraging each day; (ii) botanical composition; (iii) distance that camels move each day; and (iv) seasonal movements of camels. Through quality analyses the nutritional value of plants consumed is determined.

A typical camel herd in the Leego area varies from 15 - 100 heads. Between 4 - 20 camels give birth at any rainy season. For this research a family camel herd of about 50 camels has been chosen, and the researcher and his colleagues live with the camel owners. Data will continue to be collected for at least two wet and two dry seasons, at the beginning and end of each season to enable a comparison of diet changes. Three milking, three dry, and three male camels of approximately the same age and condition have been selected from the herd. Each camel is observed within six hours of a day. The observation time is divided into morning (up to 10 am), midday (10 am - 2 pm), and evening (2-6 pm). Two hours from each portion of the day are randomly selected for observations. Actual bite count and time spent chewing are recorded. Any other activity that occurs and the amount of time spent on it are also recorded. Four persons (the researcher and three technicians) carry out the bite account and time recording. The plants are identified on the spot and clipped for analysis. Appropriate specimens bearing leaves, flowers, fruits etc are collected, numbered and brought to the National Range Herbarium or Faculty of Agriculture Herbarium for identification control.

Plants that form part of the diet are clipped, stored in paper bags, weighed and dried in the fields for moisture analysis. This research is intended to be supplemented by some experimental studies on camel fodder plants at the field station in Yaq Bariweyne, which will start in 1988 with the assistance of Mumin Warfa. Ahmed Abdi Elmi complements his project research with doctoral studies at Utah University, USA.

Camel trypanosomiasis
Mohamed Farah Diriye, Ministry of Livestock, Forestry and Range

This subproject is a continuation of earlier research. The research area covers the interior of southern Somalia, where tabanids and other biting flies are prevalent.

Camel reproduction
Hussein M. Nuur,

This subproject has been inactive. It is gradually being reconstructed in cooperation with the Veterinary Faculty, University of Khartoum, Sudan.

Traditional veterinary medicine
Hersi Guleed, SNU; Gunnar Samuelsson, UU; Mohamed China, SNU; Set Bornstein, SVA

The purpose of this subproject is the testing of extracts of Vernonia Mogadoxensis for its efficacy as an acaricide and particularly as scabicide. Vernonia Mogadoxensis is a traditional medical plant used in Somalia against different complaints, especially gastrointestinal disorders. It is also used as an acaricide against scabies or sarcoptic mange. It has already been proved that a crude water extract was very efficient in treating scabies in goats.

Dr Gunnar Samuelsson and his group of Somali researchers are analysing and characterizing the active properties of extracts from different parts of the plant. They have also produced an extract that is tested for its acaricidal properties. The extract is tested both in vivo and in vitro test systems.

Zoonotic diseases and camels
Abdulhamid Haji Mohamed, SNU, in cooperation with Salim Haji Aliyo

This subproject is under preparation. It will link the camel project with the Veterinary Faculty, SNU.

The Family

The second part, concerning the humanistic and social sciences, consists of three activities already started during earlier phases of the project and one new topic. The subprojects are coordinated by Mohamed Said Samantar. Anders Hjort af Ornäs is adviser and consultant.

Camel management and labour migration
Mohamed Ali Hussein, SOMAC

This subproject has developed from the earlier project, "Traditional Camel Husbandry". A comprehensive pilot project has been concluded; the need is now for more formalized, more detailed, and also more localized work.

The information gathering has been based on several seasonal field trips to all the regions of the country. The main topics are: (i) livestock numbers in relation to human population; (ii) labour requirements for different activities at different times/seasons; (iii) labour migration from the pastoral areas to urban centres and the reasons for it; (iv) impact of labour shortages on the camel production system; and (v) steps/decisions taken by camel herders against labour shortage.

The items (ii), (iv) and (v) have been brought together in two different local communities. Sedentary and mobile households have been contacted during crucial periods (e.g. end of dry season, wet season, mid dry season). In addition, a wider survey has been conducted similar to the pilot project, except that the sampling is more systematic. The survey focusses on (i) and (iii) above. In connection with (i) reference is made to Hersi Guleed's work on the health and disease survey, which includes information on family sizes.

Item (iii) is only partially covered by this project. Only the pastoral areas are included. The reasons conceived *there* for labour migrations are the main topic for investigation. Much more work on migration patterns, flows of remittances, settlement patterns, time-space questions and so on has to be done to cover this topic properly. Some cooperation is sought with Mohamed Said Samantar's commercialization project, especially in connection with flows of remittances and the traders' network (which, at least hypothetically, are crucial for the evolution of migration patterns).

Camel oral tradition
Ahmed Ali Abokor, SOMAC

During this phase of the subproject a collection of Somali oral traditions on camels has been started, including views of camels in relation to farming, fishing, handicrafts and urban life. However, a pause is made so as to accommodate the scholar's further studies.

Camel marketing
Mohamed Said Samantar, SNU

This period of the subproject concerns further investigations of the domestic marketing chain from producer to consumer, in particular flows from the Bay region and adjacent areas to the Mogadishu market. Emphasis is on rural marketing, as this not only precedes all other activities in the marketing chain, but is the most under-capitalized in terms of both investment in facilities and manpower. The traditional rural marketing system works reasonably well, considering the resources available to it and the low level of infrastructure development.

The study of marketing networks has led to a range of background information needs, such as production and consumption patterns and general market activity. The actual flows of camels and camel products in commercial networks (including middlemen networks, domestic trade structures, export of live animals, meat and possible by-products) have so far been mapped. Furthermore, information on prices and price fluctuations in camel markets has been collected, including the organization of markets and identification of price determinants. Attention is also paid to the number of buyers and sellers, their structural relations, the market shares of butchers and exporters, vertical integration (centre/periphery) and a range of market performance issues.

Another important question under study is the extent to which nomadic camel pastoralism is commercialized. To elucidate this, an analysis of livestock sales by camel owners is undertaken that includes the composition of marketed livestock, seasonal variations in sales, market conditions from the herder's perspective, price relations etc.

Camels for men and women: symbolic values and domestic work
Mohamed Ali Hussein, SOMAC (temporarily)

The role of women in a camel economy might at a first glance seem marginal, since herdsmen are normally men, traders are men etc. But women are responsible for much short-distance transport, not least that of water, often with camels. The more or less private trade in camel milk to urban markets is also open to women.

By and large, the division of labour between men and women today still follows established routines. Superimposed on these are the opportunities and constraints created by the modern society with its market economy, labour demand, consumer ideology, social service, a more urban lifestyle, mass mobilization, nation building etc. Local communities are undergoing profound social changes.

The project, which is in a pilot phase, aims at better problem formulation. In the next phase, the actual research period, the focus will be on conceptual and work changes in local communities as a response to the development of the society at large.

Early domestication of the camel
Mohamed Ali Hussein, SOMAC

This is a desk study surveying available literature. The aim is to give a background sketch of the early domestication of camels in Somalia and possibly an elaboration dealing with settlement patterns.

Family health versus herd health
Mohamed Ali Hussein, SOMAC (temporarily)

This subproject is a pilot project looking into the general family health situation in camel herding communities.

The Herd and the Family

Under this heading activities are gathered that are immediately relevant to *both* "the herd", and "the family". Ahmed Mohamed Hashi is coordinator for the following subprojects:

Camel milk proteins and cheese production
Muctar Ali Mohamed, SNU, and Märtha Larsson-Raznikiewicz, SUAS

The composition of camel milk has some similarities with that of cow's milk. The availability of water is an important determinant of the composition. But whereas in the case of camels dehydration causes the water content to increase, the opposite occurs in cattle. Dehydration of the camel also decreases the fat and protein content. Milk tests also show large variation in salt, lactose and ash content. From the camel milk analyses already performed it is evident that milk delivered from twelve camels in the same region the same day showed large variations in composition. Breeds and individual variations might partly explain the results, probably also the fact that the camels were not in equilibrium after only a couple of weeks of rain. The focus in future will be cheese making from camel milk. The following research activities are undertaken:

a. The κ-casein status and the size distribution of the casein micelles and their effects on camel milk technology are investigated.
b. The curdling part of the cheese-making process is further studied, especially its dependence on the mineral and protein content, along with its composition (see above).
c. Cheese-making experiments are performed with camel milk mixed with goat, sheep, and/or cattle milk.
d. The calcium, magnesium, iron, zinc, copper, sodium potassium and phosphorus content in the ash from the twelve camels studied previously have been determined and the results will be published.

While these more specific qualities of camel milk are studied, attention is also paid to the milk's technological properties. Most of the work within this subproject is undertaken at the Faculty of Industrial Chemistry in Mogadishu where the basic equipment is available. Parts of the analyses are performed at the Swedish University of Agricultural Sciences.

Camel milk production and composition
Ahmed Mohamed Hashi, SNU

Comprehensive information on camel milk production and composition is very scanty, and estimates of total lactation yield varies from well under 800 litres to over 3,600 litres. Insufficient information on the composition of camel milk makes it impossible to calculate its nutritive qualities. The main topics dealt with in this subproject are: How much milk does the camel produce? At what stage of lactation? For how long? What is the nutritional content of the milk and to what extent can it contribute in meeting the food requirements of the pastoral household?

Three herds have been selected for continuous surveys. This differs from what has been practiced in other corresponding studies, where usually a minimum of 10 herds or flocks have been surveyed - no less than 300 animals. The limited number of herds and animals in this subproject should be interpreted as an initial effort and later on the number will be increased (cf Hersi Guleed's research).

Several levels of analysis are carried out:

(i) The lactation studies (cf "Dairy farm project" below) give clues to milk yields. The lactation curve is tentatively characterized by manipulating the mean outputs of breeding females in different stages of lactation. Data on milk yields, estimated calf consumption and/or estimated early growth rates of the calf give an idea of the maximum potential yield.

(ii) Through the milk analyses, the average chemical milk composition is determined. Emphasis is laid on how variations affect the physiochemical characteristics of camel milk. The results will be used in interdisciplinary work on nutritional and dietary qualities.

(iii) Attempts are made to carry out some crude testing between levels of productivity and other factors (physiological, environmental and managerial), and to identify differences in productivity and quality between herds, and the factors to which they may be attributed.

Herd dynamics
Mohamed Ali Hussein, SOMAC, and Anders Hjort af Ornäs, SIAS

During the on-going project period the methods worked out in earlier research are refined and the activities expanded outside southern Somalia. The methods are discussed with government rangeland authorities. The research on the spatial aspects probably resumes in 1988.

Breeds and conceptual classification
Mohamed Ali Hussein, SOMAC

This project deals with both the factual breeds and people's conceptions of these breeds. Long-term longitudinal studies have been started. The activities have focussed on:

(i) Data collection in northern Somalia.
(ii) Biometrical measurements (weight, height, other body measurements at different ages).
(iii) Milk production recording (daily lactation).
(iv) Examination of maturity age of the different types.
(v) Examination of effects of shortage of shrubs and watering frequency on the different camel types.
(vi) Examination of resistance to diseases and other factors.

CAMEL PROJECT RESEARCH STATION

The Camel Project Research Station at Yaq Bariweyne was established in the beginning of 1987 about 110 kilometres west of Mogadishu in an area with a large camel population. The nearby well is visited daily by thousands of camels. The research station will be used as a base by scholars participating in the camel research project. The site comprises a plot 500 x 500 meters. At present 200 x 200 meters is fenced and a house for accommodation and research activities has been erected. A Landrover is permanently allocated to the research station and there is also a small Daihatsu car and a motorcycle for local transport and commuting to and from Mogadishu. To guarantee a permanent supply of petrol, a stock is kept at the station, which can also easily be reached by public transport from Mogadishu.

In connection with the research station a *mobile laboratory* was created in February 1987 so as to allow basic laboratory work to be carried out in the field. Furthermore, it also allows for a permanent presence within camel raising areas. The laboratory is solar energy powered of a back-up with automobile batteries and a petrol generator.

The camel dairy farm and dairy plant. With the mobile laboratory and activities linked to it, the scene is set for a dairy farm that includes a processing plant and facilities for research on fermentation and preservation of camel milk products. The plans are mainly for milk preservation. A baseline study of the socio-economic effects of such a plant is under way, a study that will not only provide important background data for a dairy farm project, but also supplement the rural marketing studies.

The baseline study focusses on:

(i) The potential volume of milk deliveries from nomadic herds without impairing milk consumption in the households.

(ii) Seasonal variations in milk production and consumption, including the calculation of seasonal milk surpluses.

(iii) The optimal location of milk collecting points, with special attention to distances for different categories of milk producers.

(iv) Which households and groups of households are able to deliver milk.

(v) Existing milk trading patterns and the impact on these of an increased commercialization, with special reference to the involvement of women in the milk trade.

(vi) The impact of milk commercialization on control over milk animals.

(vii) The impact of milk trading on control over revenues from camel milk.

(viii) Cultural change effects of the commercialization process.

Fodder. In connection with the Camel Research Station, a plot is set aside for cultivation and study of important camel fodder plants. Trials to plant and grow some fodder plants - bushes and trees that camels like to eat - will be made here.

TRAINING

Greater emphasis has been given to training in connection with the project than originally intended. There are several different approaches:

(i) Participation by the Somali project coordinator in a course at the University of Nairobi in order to establish academic links between Somalia and Kenya.

(ii) Specialized training, especially in veterinary and milk sciences, at the Swedish University of Agricultural Sciences and the National Veterinary Institute in Uppsala, Sweden.

(iii) Supporting PhD courses for some of the project's scholars in Sweden and at some British and American universities. The philosophy here is that researchers should first gather field data before travelling to be trained.

(iv) A study course in general development theory at SIAS, Uppsala, Sweden, for those participating under (ii) and (iii).

(v) Scientific reporting: To improve the standard of research reports from the project, a six week training course in scientific reporting has been carried out. The course was held at SOMAC, Mogadishu. The work consisted of developing texts on a micro-computer. The experiences from the course show that more courses of the same character are needed in the future.

(vi) Some of the project's researchers are also advising under- and postgraduate students at SNU, i.e. when they write their theses. Ahmed Mohamed Hashi has given a training course on camels at the Faculty of Veterinary Medicine.

LIBRARY

A reference library for the project is gradually built up at SOMAC. The main part consists of a collection of articles dealing with the camel in a rather wide perspective. There are by now slightly more than 400 articles available, with a corresponding set of articles at SIAS. The collection is further developed through libraries' international loan services.

RESEARCH COOPERATION

The camel project is now in a phase when spin-off effects are beginning to be evident. Examples of different forms of cooperation include the following:

(i) In Somalia the camel project is located at SOMAC, Department of Natural Science Research. Since the whole range of subprojects are so complex, reporting is made directly to the president of SOMAC, but the other departments of SOMAC are continuously informed about the activities.

(ii) Cooperation with the Somali National University (SNU) is well established and several faculties and departments participate in the project's activities, i.e. Faculty of Veterinary Medicine and Animal Reproduction, Faculty of Industrial Chemistry, Faculty of Economics, Department of Botany , Faculty of Agriculture etc.

(iii) A well-developed cooperation exists with the Serum and Vaccine Institute, the National Range Herbarium, Ministry of Livestock, Forestry and Range, and the National Tsetse and Trypanosomiasis Control Project. Contacts have been made with the Central Rangelands Project and the camel study done within that project.

(iv) Preliminary discussions have started about research cooperation with the Inter-Governmental Authority on Drought and Development (IGADD).

(v) In Sweden the project is located at SIAS and is integrated into the research programme "Human Life in Arid Lands" based at that institute. At the Swedish University of Agricultural Sciences cooperation is with the Department of Chemistry, Department of Pathology, and Department of Obstetrics and Gynaecology. The Swedish veterinary consultant is based at the National Veterinary Institute. Cooperation concerning laboratory matters has also been established with the National Agricultural Chemistry Laboratory. As far as traditional veterinary medicine is concerned, there is close cooperation with the Department of Pharmacology at the Uppsala University.

(vi) The camel project also has contacts with several other SOMAC/SAREC projects. The Swedish coordinator has twice invited scholars from these projects for exchange of experiences concerning research cooperation and information about activities in the projects.

PUBLICATIONS

The camel project produces its own research reports called **Camel Forum**. The series consists of Working Papers and Internal Documents. The following *Working Papers* have been published:

1 Somali Academy of Sciences and Arts: Somali Camel Research Project. Research Proposal for Fiscal Years 1983/84 and 1984/85. Working Paper No 1, March 1983.
2 Anders Hjort and Gudrun Dahl: Camel articles available at SOMAC in Mogadishu 1983. Working Paper No 2, February 1984.
3 Set Bornstein: Camel Health and Disease. Working Paper No 3, February 1984.
4 Mohamed Ali Hussein: Comparative study of the relationship between family size, herd size and management among nomadic pastoralists. Working Paper No 4, April 1984.
5 Status report after 1983/84 as conceived from Sweden. Edited by Anders Hjort. Working Paper No 5, June 1984. (Restricted circulation)

6 Ahmed Mohamed Hashi: Milk Production of the Camel. Working Paper No 6, November 1984.
7 Camel Pastoralism in Somalia. Proceedings from a workshop held in Baydhabo, April 8-13, 1984. Editor: Mohamed Ali Hussein. Working Paper No 7, November 1984.
8 Muctar Ali Mohamed: A Study of the Camel Milk Composition. Working Paper No 8, January 1985.
9 Somali Academy of Sciences and Arts: Somali Camel Research Project. Research Proposal for Fiscal Years 1985/86 and 1986/87. Working Paper No 9, March 1985.
10 Christer Krokfors: Camel articles available at SOMAC in Mogadishu 1985. Working Paper No 10, February 1986.
11 Märtha Larsson-Raznikiewicz and Muctar Ali Mohamed: Analysis of the Casein Content in Camel (Camelus Dromedarius) Milk. Working Paper No 11, July 1986.
12 R. M. Watson: A Photogrammetric Sampling of Camels to Deduce the Age Structure of Their Populations in Southern Somalia. Working Paper No 12, July 1986.
13 Anders Hjort and Mohamed Ali Hussein: Camel Herd Dynamics in Southern Somalia: Long Term Development and Milk Production Implications. Working Paper No 13, August 1986.
14 Christer Krokfors: Spatial Aspects on Seasonal Distribution of Camels in Southern Somalia. Working Paper No 14, August 1986.
15 M. E. Abu Sin: Breeding and Marketing of Racing Camels in Eastern Sudan: The Case of Butana District. Working Paper No 15, September 1986.
16 Ayele Gebre Mariam: Livestock Production and its Socio-economic Importance among the Afar in North East Ethiopia. Working Paper No 16, March 1987.
17 Mohamed Ali Hussein: Emic notes on camel breeds in Somalia. Working paper No 17, March 1987.
18 Dahl, G (ed.) Communications pour le seminaire de Gao sur le dromadaire, 1985. Working paper No 18, April 1987.
19 Mohamed Ali Hussein: Traditional practices of camel husbandry in Somalia. Working paper No 19, June 1987.
20 Omar Abdulkadir Abdurahman: Pulmonary lesions among slaughtered camels in Mogadishu, Somalia. Working paper No 20, June 1987.
21 Mohamed Said Samantar: Camel Milk Supply to Mogadishu, Somalia. Working paper No 21, September 1987.

The following *working papers* are under printing:

22 Mohamed Said Samantar and Khadija Mohamed Awaleh: A Study on the Causes of the Decline of Camel Export from Somalia.
23 Hersi Guleed: Pilot study of the health of Somali camel herds.

The *internal documents* published are:

1 Report on 1985/86 and Research Proposal for 1987 and 1988.
2 Muctar Ali Mohamed: Production of milk consumption products in dairies.

Other publications

Mohamed Ali Hussein and Anders Hjort, 1986: *Survival in Arid Lands. The Somali Camel Research Project.* Uppsala.
Mohamed Ali Hussein and Anders Hjort 1986: *Att leva i torkan. Om kameler och utveckling i Somalia.* Uppsala.
Axmed Cali Abokor, 1986: *Suuganta Geela.* Uppsala.
Axmed Cali Abokor 1987: *Somali Camel Poetry.* Uppsala.
Ahmed Artan Hange: *Somali Folktales* (in press).